THE BEAUTY BEHIND THE MASK

THE
BEAUTY
BEHIND
THE MASK

Rediscovering the Books of the Bible

CHRISTOPHER R. SMITH

CLEMENTS PUBLISHING
Toronto

Published 2007 by
Clements Publishing
213-6021 Yonge Street
Toronto, Ontario
M2M 3W2 Canada
www.clementspublishing.com

On the cover: A "Carpet Page" from the *Book of Kells*. Carpet pages were purely decorative, and were so named for their resemblance to eastern carpets. This carpet page from Folio 27v of the *Book of Kells* depicts the symbols for the four evangelists: Matthew the Man, Mark the Lion, Luke the Calf (or Bull), and John the Eagle, derived from the vision of Ezekiel.

Library and Archives Canada Cataloguing in Publication Data

Smith, Christopher R.
The Beauty Behind the Mask : Rediscovering the books of the Bible / Christopher R. Smith.

Includes bibliographical references.
ISBN 1-894667-73-5

1. Bible—Numerical division. I. Title.

BS535.S545 2007   220.5'2   C2006-901133-8

Contents

Introduction 7

1. The Problem With Chapters and Verses 13

2. The Problem With Books 41

3. Non-Traditional English Bibles 71

4. *The Books of The Bible*............................... 105

   Appendix: 133
   How Literary Structures Were Identified

   Acknowledgments 146

Introduction

In the centuries after Michelangelo painted his magnificent frescoes on the ceiling of the Sistine Chapel,[1] those frescoes were covered with several successive layers of varnish. This varnish originally had a positive purpose: it was applied to preserve the paintings. In time it darkened, however, creating a brown patina that was deepened by coatings of soot and smoke from candles in the chapel. This superimposed effect conditioned how the artwork was experienced and understood in the centuries that followed; its original appearance was lost to cultural memory. But as the chapel was being cleaned in a major restoration project (finally completed in 1999 after 20 years), it was discovered that Michelangelo's original colors had actually been very bright and bold. The "beauty behind the mask" was visible once again, and his frescoes could be appreciated with something much closer to the effect he had intended.

---

1.   These frescoes were created from 1509-1512. Michelangelo later painted *The Last Judgment* on the altar wall of the chapel, and frescoes by other artists adorn the remaining walls, but I have chosen to use the ceiling paintings as an easily recognizable illustration.

The Bible is also a work of elegant beauty. The books it contains possess a beauty of form and expression that is meant to attract us to the truth it presents. (As Julie Ackerman Link has noted, God doesn't expect truth to "stand alone." "God," she writes, "adorns truth with beauty and goodness, making it into something that appeals to every aspect of our being—our hearts and souls and bodies as well as our minds."[2]) Unfortunately, over the centuries, traditional elements have been added to the biblical text, and their cumulative effect has been to cause us to see different forms in the pages of Scripture—unattractive ones—that do not draw us to the truth in the Bible. Our experience of Bible reading is thus far less satisfying and fulfilling, and far less effective in deepening our relationship with God, than it is meant to be. (This unpleasant reading experience is aggravated further when the biblical text is presented in two columns of narrow type, on pages crowded with cross-references and notes. This presentation may be considered a further element of "tradition" that masks the beauty of the Bible on a visual level, in addition to the literary masking readers must already contend with.)

All of the traditional features that have been introduced to the biblical text were originally designed to serve positive purposes. Chapter and verse divisions, for instance, were added to so that reference works such as commentaries and concordances could be created. Several of the longer biblical books were split into two or more pieces so that they could to be accommodated on scrolls of a convenient size. (And two-column typesetting, for that matter, makes Bibles more portable and affordable.) Indeed, some traditional elements, such as translation, are actually indispensable for our understanding of the Bible, and every traditional element can still be used valuably for its originally intended purpose. But the accumulation of these elements, together with our failure to recognize that they are not an integral part of Scripture itself, has brought us to a place where we are now losing far more than we are

---

2. Julie Ackerman Link, *Loving God with All My Heart* (Grand Rapids: Discover House, 2004), p. 55.

gaining by their presence. And so we need to find ways to separate and distinguish the biblical text from traditional accretions.

While the parallels between the Sistine Chapel restoration and the task of uncovering the Bible's literary beauties should be evident, this is nevertheless an imperfect analogy. The forms in the frescoes could still be recognized behind the patina, while the Bible's literary forms have been not just darkened, but distorted. An even more suitable analogy to the effect that traditional elements have on our appreciation for Scripture may therefore be to a work of glorious architecture around which scaffolding has been erected to permit repairs or to provide structural support. These are once again positive purposes. But the scaffolding unfortunately also creates a geometric grid that guides the eye around the building, directing the attention away from its architectural beauties to a mere caricature of its proportions and harmonies. And even this analogy is a limited one, since the Bible is in no need of repair, and it can stand perfectly well on its own. The scaffolding, in its case, can be quite safely dismantled.

This book is meant to serve as a companion volume to an edition of the Bible that seeks to dismantle much of the "scaffolding" that has been erected over the centuries around the biblical text. After four years of preparation and planning, the International Bible Society (IBS) is now publishing *The Books of The Bible,* a presentation of the Scriptures in Today's New International Version (TNIV).[3] In this edition, many of the traditional elements that have been embedded in the biblical text over the years are muted or eliminated, so that readers may engage the Bible with greater enjoyment and understanding. (A single-column presentation of the text on the page, without notes or cross-references, is designed to enhance the reading experience on the visual level as well.) In the chapters that follow, as I discuss the effects that traditional elements have on our understanding of Scripture, the

---

3.   Colorado Springs: International Bible Society, 2007. This edition may be obtained on line at www.ibsdirect.com or by calling (800) 524-1588.

thinking and goals behind this new edition of the Bible should become clearer. But this book is also intended to have a broader value: to help readers of any edition of the Bible discover how they can see more of the "beauty behind the mask" as they read the Scriptures, in any version or translation.

In the pages that follow I first discuss the traditional factors that are currently obscuring form and meaning in the Bible. In Chapter One, I describe the effects of the chapter and verse divisions that were added to the Bible long after its books were written. In Chapter Two I then explain how, over the centuries, some biblical books were divided, and all the books were put in a particular sequence and given certain names, and how this, too, can make it more difficult to read the Bible with understanding and enjoyment.

Publishers and editors have actually sought on previous occasions to present the Scriptures in a format that would minimize the effects of traditional elements. In Chapter Three, I describe various English-language Bibles, testaments and Scripture portions that were published in pursuit of this goal from the 1700s to the present. Many of these provided precedents and inspiration for *The Books of The Bible*. Finally, in Chapter Four, I tell how IBS assembled a Bible Design Group that worked for four years to prepare an edition of the Scriptures in a format that would be more inviting and readable precisely because it sought to respect the literary forms of the biblical books. In this final chapter I also explain how both new and current readers of the Scriptures will be able to use this new edition for personal devotions, group studies, sermon preparation and other disciplines by which we apply the teachings of God's word to our lives. (While this book is devoted primarily to the way the Scriptures are now being presented in *The Books of The Bible*, an Appendix addresses the question of how the literary divisions marked in that edition were identified.)

It has been a privilege and a pleasure for me to serve as a member of the Bible Design Group with Glenn Paauw, Gene Rubingh, John Kohlenberger, John Dunham, Paul Berry, Micah Wierenga, Lisa Anderson and Jim Rottenborn. I am inspired by their common vision for putting the living and active word of God in the hands of new and returning readers in a form that will help them encounter it in ever more life-changing ways. I appreciate their wisdom, learning, faith and joy, and I am grateful for the fellowship we have shared together. It is therefore an honor for me to be able to tell, in the pages that follow, the story of the "why" and the "how" behind *The Books of The Bible.*

The Problem With Chapters and Verses

The traditional elements that were added to the Bible over the centuries were all originally intended to serve positive purposes. Unfortunately, they now have the cumulative effect of altering the meaning and distorting the beauty of literary form and expression we would otherwise find in the Scriptures. In this chapter we will consider the elements that arguably create the most serious problems for our understanding of the Bible, if we treat them as reliable guides to form and meaning: chapters and verses.

THE HISTORY OF CHAPTERS AND VERSES

Neither the chapter divisions nor the verse divisions we know today are the work of the biblical authors. They were introduced well over a thousand years after the last books of the Bible were written, and they are only the latest in a series of systems that have been used to divide the biblical text.

From ancient times, the books of the Bible have been separated into smaller units in different ways, for various purposes. The entire Old Testament except for Psalms was divided into paragraphs or *parashoth* even before the time of Christ; these divisions were eventually standardized.[1] For example, each of the "days of creation" at the beginning of Genesis constitutes a single *parashah*; by contrast, in our Bibles, these "days" consist of three to eight verses each. The Torah was also divided into lectionary sections for use in the synagogue. In Palestine it was divided into 154 *sedarim* or weekly lessons so that it could be read out loud in its entirety over the course of three years. In Babylon, however, where the Torah was read through every year, it was instead divided into 54 parts, each of which was also called a *parashah* (even though they did not correspond to the other divisions known by that name.)[2]

The New Testament writings, for their part, were divided early in the history of their transmission into topical sections of greatly varying lengths known as *kephalaia*. These divisions were likely introduced around the fourth century and in time became standardized, so that Matthew was customarily divided into 68 *kephalaia*, Mark into 48, Luke into 83, and so forth. However, some manuscripts attest to even earlier, differing traditions; on these the *kephalaia* system has been superimposed by later hands. And Eusebius introduced a system of his own in the fourth century when he divided the gospels into parts that were listed in ten tables, or "canons," which he organized according to which gospels contained parallel accounts of the material in question.[3]

The chapter divisions we know today were introduced around the year 1200 by Stephen Langton. He was an English church leader who studied and then lectured at the University of Paris before becoming Archbishop of Canterbury. While in Paris, Langton wrote extensive biblical commentaries. He introduced his chapter divisions to an edition of the Vulgate (the Latin Bible) most likely so that he and others could cite passages more conveniently in their commentaries. Eventually these divisions

---

1.   Ersnt Würthwein, *The Text of the Old Testament*, trans. Erroll F. Rhodes (Grand Rapids: Eerdmans, 1995), p. 20.

2.   Robert H. Pfeiffer, *Introduction to the Old Testament* (New York: Harper and Brothers, 1948), p. 81.

3.   See Kurt Aland and Barbara Aland, *The Text of the New Testament*, 2nd ed., tr. Erroll F. Rhodes (Grand Rapids: Eerdmans and Leiden: E.J. Brill, 1989), pp. 252 ff.

were incorporated into manuscripts of the Hebrew Old Testament and the Greek New Testament, and later into printed Bibles.

The verse system we know today was introduced to the New Testament in 1551 by the French linguist, classical scholar and printer Robert Estienne (also known as Stephanus). In his fourth edition of the Greek New Testament, he divided the text into verses because he wanted eventually to produce a Greek concordance. (This project was finally completed after his death by his son Henry in 1594). The Old Testament had already been divided into "verses" of a sort: by the early centuries of our era, it had become necessary for those who read the Hebrew Scriptures aloud in the synagogues to pause at regular intervals to provide an Aramaic translation, since Jews generally no longer spoke Hebrew. By the year 500, the short stretches of text that were to be read before a translation was offered had become standardized and were indicated in manuscripts by a *soph pasuq* mark (:).[4] Even so, two different systems remained in use, one in Palestine and the other in Babylonia, until they were harmonized by ben Asher in the tenth century. After Stephanus versified the New Testament, similar "verses" were created in the Old Testament by numbering the stretches of text between *soph pasuq* marks in ascending order within each of the chapter divisions that Stephen Langton had introduced two hundred and fifty years earlier.

Given this history, and particularly the great distance in space, time and culture between the biblical authors and those who later added chapters and verses to their works, it is not at all appropriate to treat these additions as if they marked intentional units within the biblical text. We should not consider them reliable guides in our efforts to appreciate the Bible's form and meaning. Significant problems arise when we do.

---

4.   Pfeiffer, p. 80.

THE PROBLEMS THAT CHAPTERS AND VERSES CREATE

Chapters and Verses Keep Us from Recognizing What Kind of Literature We Are Reading

"The Bible," a friend once said to me, "looks like a bad technical manual that you don't want to read." I knew what he meant. Chapter and verse numbers in the text of Scripture create the impression that the biblical authors were all writing the same kind of document—that for some reason, they were all composing their works a sentence at a time, numbering these sentences sequentially, and then gathering them into larger numbered groups. This impression is only heightened when each verse is printed as its own separate paragraph, as is done in many editions of the Bible. Richard Moulton lamented this effect in the preface to his *Modern Reader's Bible* (which, as we shall see in Chapter Three, he edited and formatted in such a way as to minimize the chapter and verse numbering):

> We are all agreed to speak of the Bible as a supremely great litera-
> ture. Yet, when we open our ordinary versions, we look in vain for
> the lyrics, epics, dramas, essays, sonnets, treatises, which make the
> other great literatures of the world. Instead of these, the eye catches
> nothing but a monotonous uniformity of numbered sentences, more
> suggestive of an itemized legal instrument than of what we under-
> stand as literature.[5]

The way the Bible's various literary forms have been thus obscured is a serious handicap to its modern readers, because the different forms really should be read in different ways. As Gordon Fee and Douglas Stuart write in *How to Read the Bible for All Its Worth*,

> [T]o communicate His Word to all human conditions, God chose
> to use almost every available kind of communication: narrative

---

5.   Richard Moulton, "Preface," *The Modern Reader's Bible* (New York: Macmillan, 1907), p. v.

history, genealogies, chronicles, laws of all kinds, poetry of all kinds, proverbs, prophetic oracles, riddles, drama, biographical sketches, parables, letters, sermons and apocalypses. To interpret properly the ... biblical texts, ... one needs to learn the special rules that apply to each of these literary forms (genres). ... [T]he way God communicates His Word to us in the "here and now" will often differ from one form to another.[6]

Unfortunately, however, because the Bible's various literary forms have basically been homogenized by chapter and verse numbering, we are instead susceptible to reading observations as if they were promises or commands, to thinking that figurative or symbolic language is meant to be taken literally, and to making many other interpretive mistakes.

Most recent versions of the Bible strive to overcome this problem by using different formats to present the various scriptural genres appropriately on the page. Narrative is printed as prose, but poetry is printed line-by-line, genealogy in columns, and so forth. Nevertheless, the chapter and verse numberings remain within the text, and they undercut the impression that the books of the Bible should be read as whole literary works of different genres.

Chapters Don't Correspond With Books' Inherent Divisions

A second problem with chapters and verses is that they typically don't follow a book's inherent divisions. That is, they not only disguise literary form, they distort literary structure. Let us consider first the significant ways in which chapters do this, and note some of their other effects. We will then observe how traditional verse divisions also fail to correspond with the biblical writers' units of thought, and how they create further problems of their own.

We do not need to look very far into the Bible to find badly placed chapter breaks. The very first chapter division in the Bible, in fact,

---

6. Gordon D. Fee and Douglas Stuart, *How to Read the Bible For All Its Worth* (Grand Rapids: Zondervan, 1982), p. 20.

between Genesis 1 and 2, breaks up a coherent unit, dividing the seventh day of creation from the first six. This chapter break may be largely responsible for the way interpretation of this passage has come to focus on the "how" of creation (generating debates about whether the "six days" are literal, 24-hour periods) instead of the "why" of creation, expressed in the mandate for creaturely worship embodied in the seventh-day sabbath. (If this chapter break had been placed at the end of the seventh day, we may note, it would have corresponded with the start of a natural unit within the book of Genesis, the "generations of the heavens and the earth.")

Many other examples of what seem to be badly placed chapter breaks can also be cited. The break between Romans 7 and 8, for instance, separates Paul's discussion of what it is like to live under the law—to know what God expects, but not have the power to do it—from the glorious solution to this problem he then proclaims in the gospel: "the law of the Spirit who gives life has set you free from the law of sin and death." Because "Romans 7" has now been isolated, as if it were an independent treatise, from the larger discussion in which it plays a part, the condition it describes is often considered—incorrectly, I feel—to represent a normative situation for believers. But no matter how Paul's comments in Romans 7 are understood, they should not be interpreted without reference to what he writes immediately afterwards.

Badly placed chapter breaks also interfere with our understanding in many other passages that may be less well known. For example, in the book of Hebrews the break between chapters 4 and 5 has been placed shortly after the beginning of the discussion about Jesus as our high priest; the chapter break thus attaches the opening of this section to the conclusion of the preceding discussion of Jesus as "apostle." The break between Malachi 3 and 4, to cite another example, cuts that book's closing oracle in half; this break does not appear at all in the Hebrew text, in which Malachi has only 3 chapters. And the division between Nehemiah 6 and 7 splits off the end of a description of how the Jerusalem wall was completed, and attaches it to a genealogy that follows.

Beyond noting such individual examples from various parts of Scripture, we can also proceed more systematically to explore how traditional chapters typically do not correspond with the biblical books' inherent divisions. We may take up a book of the Bible, eliminate its chapter and verse divisions, and then trace the development of its argument or narrative. We can then go back and check where the chapter breaks have been placed. In many cases, we will have to conclude that their placement is quite unfortunate.

For example, when we consider Colossians without chapters and verses, we may reasonably conclude that it has three major sections. Since Paul has not met the Colossians, he begins this letter by laying down some relational and doctrinal foundations. The main body of the epistle then presents correction, followed by instruction. The letter ends, finally, with personal greetings. If, after this brief survey of its contents, we were asked to divide Colossians into four chapters of roughly equal length, we could easily identify how to create four internally coherent units of about the same size:

1. Relational and Doctrinal Foundations
2. Correction
3. Instruction
4. Personal Greetings

The traditional chapter divisions themselves create four sections of roughly equal length within the book of Colossians, and the break between chapters 2 and 3 comes right where we might expect, between "correction" and "instruction." But this is the only well-placed traditional division in the book. To illustrate how poorly placed the others are, let us consider a thematic outline of Colossians in a bit more detail, with the current chapter divisions marked by (x):

I. Relational and Doctrinal Foundations
    A. Paul's Prayer
    B. Paul's Gospel

C. Paul's (x) Struggle

II. Correction and Instruction

    A. Correction: no Spiritual Status Symbols

    (x) B. Instruction:

        1. Off with the old, on with the new

        2. Responsibilities of those in and under authority

            a. Wives and husbands

            b. Children and parents

            c. Servants (x) and masters

        3. Attitude towards outsiders/opponents

III. Concluding Greetings

We see that the break between chapters 1 and 2 actually cuts off a small part of the opening "foundations" section, grouping it with "correction." Even worse, it does not preserve intact the smaller units within this opening section, in which Paul shares first his prayer, then his gospel, then his struggle. Rather, this chapter break divides "Paul's struggle" into two parts, and groups the second with the "correction" that follows, even though a very clear transitional statement intervenes ("So then, just as you received Christ Jesus as Lord, continue to live your lives in him . . ."). How are readers to make sense of either chapter 1, which has an important piece missing at the end, or chapter 2, which begins misleadingly with the ending of a previous section? This is the equivalent of stopping a symphony two thirds of the way through its first movement and then, after a pause, playing the rest of this movement and continuing without a break into the second movement. It is, in other words, artistically absurd.

But the worst division of all is between chapters 3 and 4. It comes in the *middle* of II.B.2.c. That is, it actually breaks up a sub-sub-subsection. Dividing just one sentence later would have kept together this unit ("servants and masters") and the larger discussion of which it is a part ("responsibilities of those in and under authority"). And placing the division only a little bit farther into the book would have resulted in a very logical placement, at the end of II and the beginning of III.

So why was this chapter division put where it was? No doubt the desire was to give prominence to the command, "Masters, provide your slaves with what is right and fair." But the true meaning and impact of these words is simultaneously blunted by their confusing association with phrases later in this fourth chapter such as "devote yourselves to prayer, being watchful and thankful" and "Tychicus will tell you all the news about me." The admonition to masters may remain the most memorable part of the chapter because of its leading position. Nevertheless, because it has been isolated from the rest of the section to which it belongs, it is likely to be misunderstood as a moralism or rule, rather than as one of three examples that illustrate a principle: in Christ, authority relationships involve reciprocal responsibilities.

What is true of Colossians is true of most other biblical books as well: the chapter divisions simply do not follow their inherent development of thought. If we were to do a similar analysis of 1 Corinthians, for example, we would discover that long discussions of single topics have been broken up into chapters 1, 2, 3 and 4; into chapters 8, 9 and 10; and into chapters 12, 13 and 14. On the other hand, chapter 6 contains two separate discussions, as do chapters 7 and 11, while chapter 16 contains another short discussion plus an explanation of Paul's travel plans and some greetings. Only chapters 5 and 15 consist entirely of a single discussion. Chapter divisions, therefore, must not be accepted uncritically as necessarily offering a reliable guide to this, or any other, book's outline.

Modern publishers, it should be noted, try to overcome the effects of such badly placed chapter divisions by extending paragraphs right through them as necessary. However, our habits of reading tend to counteract the help that publishers are giving us here, since we typically study and discuss books of the Bible chapter-by-chapter anyway. And even during more informal reading, those large, bold chapter numbers still act as "stop signs," even in the middle of a paragraph.

Chapter divisions were basically introduced to the Bible to help readers locate passages, and so they are designed to be generally the same length. As a result, as we have already observed, they often break up longer sections, or else combine two or more shorter ones. Reading just a chapter at a time (whether in daily devotions, or in a weekly Bible study, or as a Scripture lesson for a sermon) therefore often forces us to treat only part of a longer section as if it were complete in itself, or else to try to find coherence in a combination of two separate sections. This cannot be done on the author's own terms, because the author never intended these sections to be divided or combined in this way.

Chapters do make sense in some books, such as Psalms, where they basically do correspond to inherent divisions, in this case between songs written on different occasions by various authors. Even in Psalms, however, the chapter divisions are not perfect. It is quite likely that Psalms 9 and 10 were originally a single psalm that has now been split in two, and that Psalms 42 and 43 were also originally just one psalm. In most other biblical books, chapters more seriously obscure, rather than illuminate, the original units of thought.

Chapters Mask the Existence of Larger Literary Units

And even when traditional chapter divisions do manage to hit the "seams" in a biblical book pretty well (as is sometimes the case), they nevertheless hinder our reading in a further way: they mask the existence of units that are of a larger size than even potentially well-divided chapters. In other words, there may be a higher level of literary organization in a biblical book, above the "chapter" level. On this level we would find larger units made up of several chapters. But because chapters always appear to be the largest units in a book, even when they're good, they're usually still bad, because they keep us from recognizing these larger units.

For example, when we examine the laws in Leviticus, we discover that they are grouped together by the subjects they treat, such as leprosy, or clean and unclean foods, or festivals. Moreover, we find that these groups of laws are often marked at their beginning or end with summary phrases that identify their content: "These are the regulations for the guilt offering" (7:1), or "So Moses announced to the Israelites the appointed festivals of the LORD" (23:44). For the most part, the chapters of Leviticus correspond well to the subject matter, in that they contain one group of laws on a given subject. A few dietary laws have not been shaved off the end of their group, for example, and included instead with the childbirth laws. These groups-of-laws are therefore among the "best" chapters in the Bible, in that they generally respect the book's inherent divisions.

Nevertheless, the chapters of Leviticus still obscure its essential structure, which actually consists of groups of groups of laws, organized according to a series of larger themes. For example, certain foods (ch. 11), childbirth (ch. 12), skin diseases (chs. 13-14), and bodily discharges (ch. 15) can all cause "uncleanness." These four groups of laws have therefore been put together in a larger section of the book that has to do with uncleanness. This "group of groups of laws" constitutes a literary division above the chapter (or "group of laws") level. As I have argued elsewhere, the book can be understood to have four such large divisions, with briefer material intervening between them.[7] But the 27 chapters into which the book has been divided represent its highest divisions in most readers' eyes, and so these readers have no opportunity to appreciate this structure or to understand the book's contents in light of it.

The chapters in Matthew similarly obscure the existence of a higher level of literary structure. As I have also argued elsewhere,[8] the material in Matthew is basically organized, at the highest level, by genre. After an opening genealogy (the list of Jesus' ancestors), the main narrative, which tells the story of Jesus' life, is repeatedly punctuated by long discourses (sermons or speeches). Five of these discourses are specially marked by an opening formula, which speaks of the disciples coming to Jesus for instruction, and also by a closing formula, "when Jesus had finished saying these things . . . ." In my analysis each of these

---

7.   Christopher R. Smith, "The Literary Structure of Leviticus," *Journal for the Study of the Old Testament* 70 (1996): 17-32.

8.   Christopher R. Smith, "Literary Evidences of a Fivefold Structure in the Gospel of Matthew," *New Testament Studies* 43 (1997): 540-551.

discourses takes up a theme, introduced in the previous narrative, that relates to the "kingdom of heaven." The gospel's core thus successively considers the foundations, mission, mystery, family and destiny of the kingdom. The gospel ends with the story of Jesus' arrest, trial, crucifixion and resurrection (all of these make up the "passion narrative").

According to this interpretation, at its highest level, Matthew would have a core made up of five narrative-discourse pairs, surrounded by introductory and concluding material:

GENEALOGY
FOUNDATIONS NARRATIVE - FOUNDATIONS DISCOURSE
MISSION NARRATIVE - MISSION DISCOURSE
MYSTERY NARRATIVE - MYSTERY DISCOURSE
FAMILY NARRATIVE - FAMILY DISCOURSE
DESTINY NARRATIVE - DESTINY DISCOURSE
PASSION NARRATIVE

There is no way to recognize this structure, however, or to understand this gospel's contents in light of it, by approaching Matthew as a book with 28 "chapters." This is true even though these chapters, once again, are pretty good, in that they typically respect the "seams" in this larger outline. The start of a discourse always begins a new chapter, for example, even if some discourses are divided into more than one chapter. The problem is that larger units in the book are being broken up and obscured by these chapters themselves.

Chapters Conceal the Existence of Smaller Literary Units

But there is another level of literary structure that chapters also obscure: the one below the chapter level. Chapters, at their best, correspond to sections of a shorter book, or to subsections of a longer book (that is, smaller divisions of that book's largest constituent parts). In Leviticus, for example, the major sections are the groups of groups of laws, and the groups of laws, to which the chapters correspond, are subsections of these. But below these sections and subsections typically lie even smaller units. The individual laws in Leviticus constitute the lowest level of organization in that book. For example, this law constitutes a unit on the that level:

> When anyone brings a grain offering to the LORD, your offering is to be of the finest flour. You are to pour olive oil on it, put incense on it and take it to Aaron's sons the priests. The priest shall take a handful of the flour and oil, together with all the incense, and burn this as a memorial portion on the altar, a food offering, an aroma pleasing to the LORD. The rest of the grain offering belongs to Aaron and his sons; it is a most holy part of the food offering presented to the LORD (Leviticus 2:1-3).

Chapters and verses obscure the existence of this level of organization as well, since chapters divide a book into larger sections, while verses divide it into smaller ones. (The law just quoted above, for example, is divided into three verses in our Bibles.) However, the problem here is not so severe as in the case of literary organization above the chapter level, since modern Bible publishers typically divide the text into sections corresponding to units on this lower level, and some even provide topical headings for each section. (Nevertheless, we as readers should still come to our own conclusions about whether these modern divisions correspond to the ones inherent in the material, and if we conclude that in some cases they do not, we should think in terms of different section divisions ourselves. For that matter, we should be aware that these topical divisions can create some of the same problems as chapters themselves, such as obscuring the existence of larger literary units, and allowing us to approach the Bible as if it represented a compendium of short devotional or lectionary selections, rather than a library of whole literary works. We should certainly not let section headings discourage us from reading the books of the Bible continuously, rather than in short fragments.)

Since many Bibles already do contain some indications of literary structure below the chapter level, the greater challenge before us as readers and students of the Scriptures is to recognize and appreciate the higher levels of organization in biblical books. This challenge has already been discussed in some books on effective Bible reading. The phenomenon of higher and lower levels of organization, above and below chapters, has been highlighted, for example, by Grant Osborne. In a short section of *The Hermeneutical Spiral: A Comprehensive Introduction to Biblical Interpretation,* Osborne stresses the importance of what he calls "charting a book." He writes,

> We must remember that verse and chapter divisions were never inspired. . . . The problem is that [scribes] often chose both verse and chapter divisions poorly, yet people tend to assume that [their] decisions were correct and interpret verses and chapters apart from the context around them.[9]

(The problem may also be that people don't realize these divisions aren't the work of the original authors.) Osborne argues that we should instead seek to trace the "thought development" of the whole book, and produce an outline that identifies its "major units."

In the same way, Kay Arthur, in *How to Study Your Bible*, briefly instructs readers to identify the level of organization above chapters, and to describe the "segments" or "major divisions" in a book of the Bible. She warns, "You don't subjectively create segment divisions. Rather, you discover them from the text."[10] She also trains readers to look for units smaller than chapters. She warns that these may not correspond to the publisher's paragraph divisions, and that they may run across the traditional chapter divisions, which, like the publisher's, are "man made," and can be misleading.[11]

---

9. Grant Osborne, *The Hermeneutical Spiral: A Comprehensive Introduction to Biblical Interpretation* (Downers Grove, Illinois: InterVarsity Press, 1991), p. 23.

10. Kay Arthur, *How to Study Your Bible: The Lasting Rewards of the Inductive Approach* (Eugene, Oregon: Harvest House, 1994), p. 40.

11. Ibid., p. 53. However, in light of what we have seen here about the problem that chapter divisions generally can create for our understanding of the Bible, we must be less appreciative of another part of Arthur's approach: she also encourages readers to

Unfortunately, such disciplined habits are not typical of the way most of us now read or study the Scriptures. Instead, it is much more common for us to approach the Bible through its traditional chapter divisions. Home study groups often take up a chapter a week; ministers doing expository series typically preach through a book chapter by chapter; personal Bible reading schedules often prescribe a certain number of chapters a day. In fact, while we probably often feel a little uncomfortable or even guilty with the way we quote verses (asking ourselves, "Might this be a 'text out of context that's really a pretext'?"), we tend to consider chapter-based approaches much more rigorous and trustworthy. We need to be aware, therefore, of all the ways in which the traditional chapter divisions inhibit our ability to understand form, and thus meaning, as we read the Bible.

Verses Typically Do Not Correspond With the Smallest Meaningful Units

Verse divisions create even further problems for our understanding of literary structure in the Bible. For one thing, just as chapters typically fail to correspond with the intermediate-sized units in biblical books, even though they are often about the same size, so verses, which are typically of sentence length, tend not to respect the sentence-sized divisions of thought within the biblical writings. Anyone who has been reading the Bible for even a short time has no doubt noticed many individual examples of how verse divisions can break up sentences and phrases that belong together, or else combine those that should be kept separate.

The statements in 1 Corinthians 6:19-20, for example, if divided reasonably into two verses, would read something like this:

---

study a book of the Bible chapter by chapter, and to write chapter summaries. It seems more consistent with her own stated goals and methods to invite her readers instead to discern "sub-segments," between "segments" and "paragraphs," and to study these in place of chapters.

(19) Do you not know that your bodies are temples of the Holy Spirit, who is in you, whom you have received from God?
(20) You are not your own; you were bought at a price. Therefore honor God with your bodies.

Unfortunately, the traditional verse divisions have actually been placed in these locations instead:

(19) Do you not know that your bodies are temples of the Holy Spirit, who is in you, whom you have received from God? You are not your own;
(20) you were bought at a price. Therefore honor God with your bodies.

In Psalm 42-43, to cite another example, a refrain is repeated three times:

Why, my soul, are you downcast?
    Why so disturbed within me?
Put your hope in God,
    for I will yet praise him,
my Savior and my God.

In its second and third occurrences, this refrain makes up a single verse. But in its first occurrence, the words "and my God" are divided off from the end of the last line and assigned to the following verse. (The TNIV has prudently adjusted the placement of the verse number in this case, for the sake of consistency.)

Many individual examples can also be provided of how verses combine sentences and phrases that should be kept separate. At one point in 1 Corinthians, for example, the apostle Paul wants to show that as believers, we are free not to insist on our rights in order to help further the gospel. He first establishes that he and his fellow apostles have the right to be paid for their work. Then, in a major transition, he reminds the Corinthians, "But we did not use this right." However, the fact that a major transition is occurring here is obscured because no new verse is begun. First Corinthians 9:12 combines this transitional statement with the end of the preceding part of Paul's argument:

> If others have this right of support from you, shouldn't we have it all the more? But we did not use this right. On the contrary, we put up with anything rather than hinder the gospel of Christ.

(Most modern publishers, it should be noted, put a paragraph break in the middle of this verse, to help readers follow what is happening in Paul's argument.)

These are only a few of the numerous examples that could be given to illustrate how, in individual instances, the traditional verse divisions inappropriately divide or combine sentences and phrases. But we should note further that verse divisions can also distort our understanding of how a longer passage's component sentences and phrases function within it. For example, the Ten Commandments, cited here from Exodus 20:1-17, would be divided most logically as follows, one commandment per verse:

> And God spoke all these words: I am the LORD your God, who brought you out of Egypt, out of the land of slavery.
>
> 1 You shall have no other gods before me.
> 2 You shall not make for yourself an idol in the form of anything in heaven above or on the earth beneath or in the waters below. You shall not bow down to them or worship them; for I, the LORD your God, am a jealous God, punishing the children for the sin of the parents to the third and fourth generation of those who hate me, but showing love to a thousand generations of those who love me and keep my commandments.
> 3 You shall not misuse the name of the LORD your God, for the LORD will not hold anyone guiltless who misuses his name.
> 4 Remember the Sabbath day by keeping it holy. Six days you shall labor and do all your work, but the seventh day is a Sabbath to the LORD your God. On it you shall not do any work, neither you, nor your son or daughter, nor your manservant or maidservant, nor your animals, nor any foreigner residing in your towns. For in six

days the LORD made the heavens and the earth, the sea, and all that is in them, but he rested on the seventh day. Therefore the LORD blessed the Sabbath day and made it holy.

5 Honor your father and your mother, so that you may live long in the land the LORD your God is giving you.

6 You shall not murder.

7 You shall not commit adultery.

8 You shall not steal.

9 You shall not give false testimony against your neighbor.

10 You shall not covet your neighbor's house. You shall not covet your neighbor's wife, or his manservant or maidservant, his ox or donkey, or anything that belongs to your neighbor.

However, our current system of versification instead divides the Ten Commandments this way:

1 And God spoke all these words.

2 I am the LORD your God, who brought you out of Egypt, out of the land of slavery.

3 You shall have no other gods before me.

4 You shall not make for yourself an idol in the form of anything in heaven above or on the earth beneath or in the waters below.

5 You shall not bow down to them or worship them; for I, the LORD your God, am a jealous God, punishing the children for the sin of the parents to the third and fourth generation of those who hate me,

6 but showing love to a thousand generations of those who love me and keep my commandments.

7 You shall not misuse the name of the LORD your God, for the LORD will not hold anyone guiltless who misuses his name.

8 Remember the Sabbath day by keeping it holy.

9 Six days you shall labor and do all your work,

10 but the seventh day is a sabbath to the LORD your God. On it you shall not do any work, neither you, nor your son or daughter, nor your manservant or maidservant, nor your animals, nor any foreigner residing in your towns.

11 For in six days the LORD made the heavens and the earth, the sea, and all that is in them, but he rested on the seventh day. Therefore the LORD blessed the Sabbath day and made it holy.

12 Honor your father and your mother, so that you may live long in the land the LORD your God is giving you.

13 You shall not murder.

14 You shall not commit adultery.

15 You shall not steal.

16 You shall not give false testimony against your neighbor.

17 You shall not covet your neighbor's house. You shall not covet your neighbor's wife, or his manservant or maidservant, his ox or donkey, or anything that belongs to your neighbor.

At least some of the force of the Ten Commandments derives from the fact that 10 is the number of humanity in the Bible and in popular understanding (people typically having 10 fingers and 10 toes). Indeed, the Decalogue is not so much a list of rules as it is a call for humans, as humans, to acknowledge the worship and obedience they owe to God as Creator ("the LORD made the heavens and the earth") and Redeemer ("your God, who brought you out of Egypt"). In other words, the form of the Decalogue is meant to help us understand its purpose. But this form is obscured when it is divided into seventeen parts.

Verses Encourage Disintegrative Approaches to the Bible

Other kinds of problems also arise when verses are treated as independent statements, as their numbering misleadingly suggests they should be. For one thing, they permit and even encourage disintegrative approaches to the reading and study of the Bible.

One of my parishioners once invited me over to see the new Bible program he had just gotten for his home computer. As I looked on, he proudly showed me its many features. One of these was a search-by-topic function. The computer presented an alphabetized list of subjects on which we could consult the Bible. By clicking on a word, we could get a series of verses to appear on-screen dealing with that topic. This list was alphabetical, beginning with A, and so the first word was "alcohol." That seemed as good a place to begin as any, so I asked my friend to click on that word. The computer soon printed out a list of Bible verses on the subject of alcohol, such as:

"Do not get drunk on wine, which leads to debauchery. Instead, be filled with the Spirit" (Ephesians 5:18).

"Wine is a mocker and beer a brawler; whoever is led astray by them is not wise" (Proverbs 20:1).

"Who has woe? Who has sorrow? Who has strife? Who has complaints? Who has needless bruises? Who has bloodshot eyes? Those who linger over wine, who go to sample bowls of mixed wine" (Proverbs 23:29-30).

The many other verses the computer also selected were all along these same lines. I looked over the list for a while and finally said, "You know, they left out a few."

My friend asked, "What do you mean?"

I replied, "Just look at the list."

Pretty soon a grin broke over his face and he said, "Oh yes," and recited, "Stop drinking only water, and use a little wine for the sake of your stomach" (1 Timothy 5:23). My friend recognized that while the computer had been programmed to list only verses that warned against the abuse of alcohol (certainly a very important warning to provide), the Bible also contains statements that alcohol can have a positive use, such as the one he remembered. I mentioned another, the reference in Psalm 104 to God bringing forth from the earth "wine that gladdens human hearts, oil to make their faces shine, and bread that sustains their hearts."

But there were other verses we could have cited, of an even different character. When we search its pages, we discover that the Bible actually contains some statements about alcohol that are very troubling. For example, God commands the Israelites in Deuteronomy 14:25-26, "[E]xchange your tithe for silver, and take the silver with you and go to the place the LORD your God will choose. Use the silver to buy whatever you like: cattle, sheep, wine or other fermented drink, or anything you wish." Are we really to spend our tithe on liquor? There is an even more disturbing statement in Proverbs 31:6-7: "Let beer be for those who are perishing, wine for those who are in anguish! Let them drink and forget their poverty and remember their misery no more." Does God really countenance people escaping from their problems through drunkenness? And does God want us to encourage this behavior on the part of the poor, rather than helping them escape from poverty?

Not really. When we read the verses just quoted in light of their surrounding argument, we discover that there is genuine concern for the poor in this passage, and that the Bible is not condoning drunkenness. The larger context reads:

> It is not for kings, Lemuel—
> not for kings to drink wine,
> not for rulers to crave beer,
>
> lest they drink and forget what has been decreed,
> and deprive all the oppressed of their rights.
>
> Let beer be for those who are perishing,
> wine for those who are in anguish!
>
> Let them drink and forget their poverty
> and remember their misery no more.
>
> Speak up for those who cannot speak for themselves,
> for the rights of all who are destitute.
>
> Speak up and judge fairly;
> defend the rights of the poor and needy. (Proverbs 31:4-9)

The real teaching here, in other words, is that kings should not get drunk, because if they do, they will pervert justice, and the poor and needy will not be helped. The two verses that were selected earlier from this argument are actually a rhetorical flourish within the longer passage. They are saying, in effect, "Hey, if anybody's got to get drunk, let it be those with something to forget, not those who have to stay sharp for everyone's sake." But it is not a valid inference, from this rhetoric, that anybody's really got to get drunk.

33

In the same way, by studying the tithe regulations in Deuteronomy, we could show that it would not really be proper for Christians today to spend their tithe on liquor for a party. Just as importantly, however, if we were to study more carefully the verses the computer selected, we would see that they don't really present an imperative for total abstinence from alcohol, as the search results could be taken to imply. Rather, they warn against the abuse of alcohol: "don't *get drunk* . . . don't *tarry long* over wine . . . don't be *led astray* by it." Total abstinence is still a personal conviction that many Christians will reach and observe as a way of genuinely honoring God. Nevertheless, the Bible's counsel concerning alcohol use is essentially that in this area, as in all areas of life, we should cultivate the character quality of self-control, whether this means abstinence or sober moderation.

How, then, might this computer program have left the impression that the Bible's counsel is total abstinence? By selecting and arranging certain verses. If this was done deliberately, it was no doubt done with the best of intentions. There is a long-standing and well-respected tradition of abstinence teaching in many churches. The Bible itself tells us that one may abstain as a matter of personal conviction and sensitivity to the weaknesses of others: "It is better not to eat meat or drink wine or to do anything else that will cause your brother or sister to fall" (Romans 14:21). Nevertheless, we must insist that verses should not be selected and arranged to create the impression that a matter of personal conviction or traditional emphasis is the Bible's counsel to everyone.

Indeed, verses should not be selected and arranged to create the impression that the Bible teaches anything it actually doesn't. But because verses divide the Bible up into little "sound bites," which are numbered and thus can be located and cited without regard to their context, they practically invite us to select and arrange them in support of our favorite teachings, whether or not their context actually supports the meaning we are imputing to them.

Verses Invite Us to Supply Meanings from Our Own Experience

Treating verses as intentional independent units encourages other unreliable approaches to the Bible as well. Because we typically encounter verses as isolated phrases, we tend to understand their meaning by reference to our own experience, rather than in light of their original context.

For example, in one adult Sunday School class I taught, we were discussing Jesus's statement that God "sends rain on the righteous and the unrighteous" (Matthew 5:45). The members of the class took "rain" as a reference to the problems of life, since this is what it usually means to us—as, for example, in the popular saying, "Into every life a little rain must fall." And so the class began to talk about about why bad things happen to good people. But as we looked at Matthew more closely, we realized that the "rain" Jesus was talking about here was actually a good thing: together with the sun, it brings about a good harvest. The real question, therefore, at least for readers of this passage, should have been, "Why do good things happen to bad people?" (The short answer is, "Because God is kind.") If we really wanted to know why bad things happen to good people, we needed to look elsewhere in the Scriptures.

We probably quote verses in such a way that their meaning will be understood in light of our own experience, rather than in light of their context, far more often than we realize or would want to admit. One year at Christmas time, for example, a friend of mine went into a Christian bookstore and saw a large banner that read, "Celebrate by sending each other gifts, Revelation 11:10." That sounded like a wonderful thought for the season until she looked this statement up in her Bible and discovered that it was actually a description of how the enemies of God will rejoice over the death of the "two witnesses": they will "refuse them burial," and "the inhabitants of the earth will gloat over them and will celebrate by sending each other gifts"! Many other examples like this could be given, but the point should be clear: verses not only encourage selection and arrangement, they encourage non-contextual reading so that the reader, not the text, supplies the meaning in the end.

In fact, even when we understand the meaning of the words in an isolated statement the way they would have been understood in their original historical context, we may still misunderstand the statement because we fail to appreciate it within its literary context, that is, within the author's own developing argument. We saw an example of this earlier: the statement "let beer be for those who are perishing . . . let them drink and forget their poverty" is not a positive command for us to ply the poor with liquor. It is simply a contrast that is being drawn to make the point that "it is not for kings to drink wine, not for rulers to crave beer." In other words, verses break up the thoughts of the biblical authors, causing us to understand them incompletely and often to misunderstand them.

Verses Can Create the Impression That the Bible Is Ambiguous

There is yet another problem with treating verses as intentional units: this can actually prevent the Bible from being a reliable source of guidance. Verses can be pitted against one another to suggest that there is really no clear path for a person to follow in life. In other words, a verse-by-verse approach creates the impression that the Bible's teaching is ambiguous.

I was visiting a friend's church one Sunday when the special feature was a puppet show. In it, a boy named Billy was concerned because his father had lost his job. At one of Billy's shoulders stood a devil puppet, who was trying to convince him that God didn't want his father to get a new job. To strengthen his many arguments, the devil puppet asked, "Doesn't the Bible say, 'Blessed are you who are poor?'" (Luke 6:20). At the other shoulder was an angel puppet, who countered that Billy should take his concerns to God in prayer. This angel quoted from Paul's letter to the Philippians: "Do not be anxious about anything, but in every situation, by prayer and petition, with thanksgiving, present your requests to God. And the peace of God, which transcends all understanding, will guard your hearts and your minds in Christ Jesus" (Philippians 4:6-7). As soon as Billy heard the angel say this, he prayed, and experienced the peace of

Christ. All of us in the audience nodded in approval. (And eventually, Billy's father did get a job.)

This was a wonderful lesson for the children for whom the puppet show was intended, and for the rest of us: we should trust God and pray in troubling times. But on what basis did Billy, and we, know that prayer was the right thing for him to do in his family's situation? The devil and the angel were actually using the same approach to the Bible—quoting verses. So how was Billy to know whether he should just accept the situation and be grateful for the spiritual blessings his family was about to receive through poverty ("blessed are you who are poor"), or try to change the situation, making his requests known through intercessory prayer? He, and we, may have come to our conclusion through experience; we may have been unemployed ourselves at some point, and so didn't think it was something God would have wanted for Billy's father, at least not on a long-term basis. Or, we might have remembered the many times we in our churches had prayed for people who needed jobs. We might even have known that the devil puppet was actually quoting Luke 6:20 out of context. Jesus doesn't say there that the poor are blessed because they are in want, but rather because they are not in a place of earthly privilege that makes them resistant to the gospel. But neither we nor Billy could have reached the right conclusion from relating to the Bible on the verse level, because on that level, it's ambiguous. Luke 6:20 and Philippians 4:6-7, considered as isolated statements, point in opposite directions for someone in Billy's situation. And if we never leave the verse level, this ambiguity can only be resolved by something other than the Bible. When this happens, the Bible ceases to be our primary authority; something else inevitably takes its place.

In other words, when we take "Bible verses" as statements that can meaningfully stand alone, apart from their context, this allows and even encourages us to develop bad habits of reading and study. These bad habits can ultimately lead us to substitute our own teachings and understandings for those of the Bible. This happens in several ways: through selection and arrangement; through reading in isolation; and in response to the impression that the Bible's counsel is ambiguous.

37

Verses Encourage Legal and Propositional Readings of the Bible

Furthermore, even when we do not substitute our own teachings for those in Scripture, verses may encourage us to understand even the Bible's teachings in unbiblical ways. Verses encourage us to read one statement at a time, and thus foster legal and intellectual readings of the Bible, as if it essentially contained rules for us to follow, or doctrines to which we should assent. But obeying the Bible's teachings does not mean following a set of rules or embracing a set of beliefs. Rather, because the Bible is essentially seeking to introduce us to God, obeying the Bible's teaching means, before anything else, entering into a personal relationship with God, and then having our minds and characters transformed as that relationship with God grows and deepens.

CONCLUSION

We have seen how the division of the biblical text into the short snippets represented by verses encourages bad habits of reading that lead to irresponsible use of the Scriptures. All of this would be bad enough even if verses managed to respect the sentence-level divisions of thought within the biblical writings. But, as we have seen, they typically do not.

Given all of these problems with verses, we should be very concerned about the extent to which many of us actually relate to the Bible on the verse level, in addition to the ways we approach it through traditional chapter divisions. We rely on the topical lists of verses that we find not only in computer programs like my friend's, but also in "pocket promise books" or in the front or back sections of our Bibles. We memorize the Bible, from our earliest days in Sunday School, a verse at a time (carefully learning the numbered reference as well). In our homes we have wall plaques, posters, calendars and even coffee mugs that daily present Bible verses to us. The sermons we hear in church may send us flipping back and forth through the pages of our Bibles to find the verses being cited in support of specific points. In the process, we may be using a translation that prints each verse as a separate paragraph. Even scholarly commentaries, written by interpreters who are well aware that the original authors did not divide their works into chapters and verses, tend to go chapter-by-chapter and verse-by-verse through biblical books anyway, if only so that their readers may turn conveniently to their comments on a particular passage. Indeed, it may be more common for believers to approach the Bible on the verse level than in any other way. But so long as we continue this approach, we are permitting and perhaps even encouraging ourselves and others to substitute human "traditions and teachings" for the Bible's own counsel. We are not hearing genuinely from God, and we are not having a life-changing encounter with God through the Word. No wonder our experience of Scripture is not satisfying and enjoyable; no wonder it does not keep us coming back for more. We therefore need to approach the Bible in a new way.

If we want to understand the Bible on its own terms, we should relate to it properly not on the verse level, nor on the chapter level, but on the level of its individual books, particularly if we can set aside the signals being sent by chapters and verses and appreciate the multi-layered literary structures the biblical books actually have. The Bible is, after all, essentially a collection of literary creations. Their "book form" is thus their original form. However, we should also note that traditional elements create some problems for those who approach the Bible even on the book level. We will explore these in our next chapter.

2

The Problem with Books

When Luke and Acts are read together, it becomes evident that they are united by an overarching literary structure. As L. T. Johnson observes, the author of these volumes

> uses geography to structure his story and to advance his literary
> and theological goals. . . . In the Gospel, the narrative moves *toward*
> Jerusalem. . . . In Acts, the geographic movement is *away from*
> Jerusalem. . . . The middle twelve chapters of the two-volume work
> narrate events exclusively in that place.[1]

In other words, a symmetrical "journey to Jerusalem/journey from Jerusalem" structure unites Luke and Acts into a single work. This is a two-volume historical study whose purpose is to permit believers such as the commissioning patron Theophilus (who is acknowledged at the start of each volume) to "know the certainty of the things you have been taught" regarding the ministry of Jesus and his followers.

---

1.   Luke Timothy Johnson, *The Gospel of Luke*, Sacra Pagina 3 (Collegeville, Minn.: Liturgical Press, 1991), pp. 14-15.

It is appropriate for there to be some kind of division between Luke and Acts, since the author himself, in his second dedication to Theophilus, refers back to the first volume as his *protos logos*, or the "first section"[2] of his historical narrative. But the two parts should nevertheless be read together, as a whole literary work. Unfortunately, because they are no longer attached to one another, they are instead not just read separately, but approached as if they were "different books," in the sense of having been written for different purposes on different occasions. An awareness of the structural and thematic unity they possess as component parts of a single work, an awareness that would inform and enrich a reading of each volume, is thereby lost.

The impression that Luke and Acts are different books is heightened by the way that John, an entirely separate composition by another author, intervenes between them. This placement of John actually serves to associate Luke more with that book, and with Matthew and Mark, than with Acts itself. A group of "gospels" has been created, from which Acts has been separated out as "history." In other words, readers who might otherwise approach Luke-Acts as a whole literary creation are misdirected not just by the division of that two-volume work into distinct parts, but by the traditional sequence and grouping of the books of the Bible, which moves them apart and actually assigns one volume to a collection of writings from which the other is excluded.

Beyond even this, tradition has also assigned dissimilar titles to the two volumes of this historical study, and these titles strongly reinforce the impression that Luke and Acts are different kinds of literature. The first volume's full traditional title is "The Gospel of Luke" or "The Gospel According to Luke"; this implies that it belongs to a "gospel" genre. The second volume, on the other hand, has been entitled "The Acts of the Apostles," suggesting that it is a work that relates the "acts" of a notable

---

2.   According to Liddell and Scott, the term *logos* was used to refer to one section of a historical work; in the plural, it meant a full "chronicle" or an ordered collection of such historical accounts. *Greek-English Lexicon* (Oxford: Clarendon Press, 1968), p. 1058.

person or persons. This is a well-attested genre of Greco-Roman litera-ture. David Aune, in *The New Testament in Its Literary Environment,* notes such examples as Callisthenes' *Acts of Alexander* and Sosylus' *Acts of Hannibal.* Aune concludes, however, that "[t]he term offers little help in determining the genre of the book of Acts." Instead, he suggests, Luke's most influential model for this work was provided by the "general history," which "focused on the history of a particular people . . . from mythical beginnings to a point in the recent past."[3] Luke's "general history," comprising both volumes, would be of the inbreaking kingdom of God, starting with the events surrounding the birth of Jesus. We should therefore not consider Acts, either structur-ally or thematically, to be a book that essentially relates first the "acts" of Peter, then those of Philip, and then those of Paul, even though its traditional title would encourage us to do this. It is rather the continu-ation of a "general history" that begins in Luke.

In summary, then, the traditional divisions, sequence and grouping of the biblical books encourage us to read Luke's two-volume work as if represented separate books that are different kinds of literature. If we are ever to appreciate the actual form and meaning of this work, we must resist the signals we are getting from all of these traditional factors.

Luke-Acts provides probably the clearest example of the effects of the book-level traditional factors we will be considering in this chapter. We concluded in our last chapter that we should approach the Bible most properly on the book level, not on the chapter or verse level. Doing this will probably require a new discipline on our parts, since we are so used to navigating by chapters and verses, which provide what feels like "instant access" to Scripture. Starting at the book level, on the other hand, requires us to put in some time of preparatory work as we read and study individual books. We should properly consider them in their

---

3. David Aune, *The New Testament in Its Literary Environment,* Library of Early Christianity 8 (Philadelphia: Westminster Press, 1987), p. 78.

entirety before taking up individual sections. Beyond this, as we will see in more detail now, we also need to be aware of, and compensate for, the way certain traditional elements actively obscure form and meaning even on the book level.

These traditional elements, which we have just seen illustrated in the case of Luke-Acts, are once again: the way some longer books have been divided into two or more parts; the sequence in which we are now accustomed to encountering the books of the Bible; and the titles that tradition has assigned to these books. These elements, singly and in combination, can promote interpretations that would not otherwise arise from a reading of the simple text of a book. Specifically, they can encourage debatable assumptions on significant interpretive questions such as those of a book's authorship, intended audience, circumstances of composition, and central focus. They can also keep us from recognizing a book's literary genre and structure. As we now consider each of these three traditional factors in further detail, we will become more aware of their effects and of how we may work to overcome them.

BOOK BOUNDARIES

Book boundaries—indications of where one book ends and another begins—are one traditional factor that can obscure form and meaning in the Bible. We should not regard all of the book boundaries we are familiar with as authoritative. In some cases they, like chapters and verses, arguably do not correspond with the literary designs of the biblical authors.

We saw earlier how chapter divisions can obscure the existence of larger literary units within biblical books. In the same way, some of the traditional book divisions in the Bible obscure the existence of significant literary units—originally unified compositions, in fact—that now encompass two or more "books." This situation was created over time as several of the longer Old Testament works were divided into parts so that they could be accommodated conveniently on the scrolls of their day. These parts have now come to be treated as complete books in themselves. But they really should not be understood this way. Instead, we should situate these parts back within their fuller original literary context, in order to understand and appreciate them as we were intended to.

The case of the Old Testament books that were divided because of limitations on scroll length is somewhat different from that of Luke-Acts, which was intentionally written in two volumes. Nevertheless, if reading Luke and Acts separately creates all of the problems for our understanding that were suggested at the beginning of this chapter, then there is even less warrant to read the now-divided parts of originally whole Old Testament books separately, as if they were entire in themselves. As in the case of Luke-Acts, when we read these books in parts, we fail to observe the overarching literary-structural patterns that tie them together, which should guide our reading and understanding.

A single literary structuring pattern, for example, runs through the "books" we now know as 1 and 2 Samuel and 1 and 2 Kings. These are actually the four parts into which an originally unified composition, which we may call Samuel-Kings, has been divided. A first division was made of the Hebrew original into two books (which still appear as "Samuel" and "Kings" in Hebrew Bibles today). A later division of each of these books into two parts was made when they were translated into Greek and their text expanded by one-third, once again outstripping the convenient limits of scroll length.

The structuring pattern that ties all four of these parts together is established by a series of notices about kings and their reigns. A typical example is, "David was thirty years old when he became king, and he reigned forty years. In Hebron he reigned over Judah seven years and six months, and in Jerusalem he reigned over all Israel and Judah thirty-three years" (2 Samuel 5:4-5). The pattern, in other words, is that we are first told how old a king was when he came to the throne, and then for how many years he ruled, and in what place. These notices come either at the beginning or the end of descriptions of each king's character and the notable events and achievements of his reign. These descriptions vary greatly in length; the reigns of Saul, David and Solomon

45

particularly are considered in much more detail than those of the other kings. These regnal accounts, marked at their beginning or end by this recurring formula, constitute the largest literary units out of which an originally unified work was composed. We should not let the fact that we now encounter this material in four separate "books," a separation accentuated by a difference in names (Samuel vs. Kings), keep us from recognizing that it was all originally a single composition.

Indeed, we should recognize that the book divisions we are currently familiar with actually do not respect the inherent units within this original composition (just as chapter divisions often do not correspond with meaningful units within books). The break between 1 and 2 Samuel comes a little bit before the regnal notice that identifies Ish-Bosheth as successor to his father Saul (2 Samuel 2:10). Similarly, the break between 2 Samuel and 1 Kings comes a little before the notice that concludes David's reign (1 Kings 2:10-11). (However, a small minority tradition places the break right after this notice instead, respecting its function as a structural divider.[4]) And 2 Kings starts a little bit after the notice that begins the account of Ahaziah's reign (1 Kings 22:51). In other words, if these traditional book divisions had been placed just a little bit earlier or later, they could have coincided in each case with the regnal notices that structure the whole work. Why, then, were they placed where they were? There seems to be one explanation in the case of the earlier division of the whole work into Samuel and Kings, and another for the later division of Samuel and Kings into two parts each.

2 Samuel begins, "After the death of Saul," and 2 Kings begins, "After Ahab's death." This is reminiscent of the way Joshua begins, "After the death of Moses" and Judges begins, "After the death of Joshua." In other words, when Samuel and Kings were each divided in half after being translated into Greek, how they were divided may have been influenced by what was perceived to be a suitable literary model from Joshua and

---

4.   See the textual notes in *Septuaginta* (Stuttgart: Deutsche Bibelgesellschaft, 1979) at 2 Sam. 24:24 and 1 Kings 2:11.

Judges. But the references to the deaths of Saul and Ahab at the start of 2 Samuel and 2 Kings do not really function structurally in the same way the references to the deaths of Moses and Joshua do at the start of the books of Joshua and Judges. We should therefore not look to these death notices in Samuel-Kings as literary-structural guides, even though they now represent "first lines" of "books."

And how was it earlier determined where Samuel-Kings would be divided? A break seems to have been placed at a point where there is a pause, even though not a full stop, in this long story of the Israelite monarchy. Before the circumstances of David's death are related at what is now the beginning of Kings, some material is included recapitulating David's displacement of the house of Saul. This material is actually arranged in an ABCCBA chiasm:

A Guilt upon Israel because of Saul (21:1-14)
   B David's mighty men (21:15-22)
      C A song of David (22:1-51)
      C A song of David (23:1-7)
   B David's mighty men (23:8-39)
A Guilt upon Israel because of David (24:1-25)

(The parallel between the two "A" sections is reinforced by a repeated phrase: the first account ends, "After that, God answered prayer in behalf of the land," and the second account concludes, "Then the LORD answered [David's] prayer in behalf of the land, and the plague on Israel was stopped.") This chiastic presentation of largely non-narrative material does create an artful pause in the story. Nevertheless, we should still recognize that placing a book break at this pause makes it more difficult to recognize the literary structuring pattern that runs through all of Samuel-Kings, a pattern that should help us understand and interpret all of the material it structures as an originally unified composition.

Chronicles is another book that was divided in two when it was translated into Greek; in the Hebrew Scriptures it remains a single book. And like Samuel and Kings, Chronicles itself is only part of an even longer work, whose other part has also been divided into two books: Ezra and

Nehemiah. (They were not divided from one another in the Septuagint, but only later in the Vulgate.) We can tell that Chronicles and Ezra-Nehemiah should be seen as a single composition by the way they have been "stitched together" by the verbatim repetition of an extended excerpt from the Edict of Cyrus at the end of Chronicles (2 Chronicles 36:22-23); the Edict at full length constitutes the opening words of Ezra-Nehemiah (Ezra 1:1ff). (Analogously, some manuscripts of the Septuagint "stitch together" the separated parts of Samuel-Kings by repeating the opening words of one part at the end of the preceding one. This occurs in various manuscripts between 1 and 2 Samuel, 2 Samuel and 1 Kings, and 1 and 2 Kings. It also occurs at the break between 1 and 2 Chronicles.)

When we read Chronicles-Ezra-Nehemiah as a single work, we recognize that it is essentially a "temple history." That is, even though it tells the story of the covenant people going all the way back to Adam, its particular concern is with the temple that God commanded to be built in Jerusalem, which was rebuilt there after the exile. (The temple and its worship are the specific focus of much of the material that is presented in this work but absent from Samuel-Kings.) Worship must be offered at this temple, this work insists, and at no other, so that God may be honored in the way that God himself has chosen. But this overall emphasis is difficult to appreciate now that the work has been divided into four parts that have three different titles, particularly since two of the titles suggest that their focus is on the careers of individuals (Ezra and Nehemiah).

There is also a single literary structuring pattern that begins early in Exodus, runs all the way through Leviticus, and extends nearly to the end of Numbers. It should not surprise us that such a pattern should tie all of this material together, since Exodus, Leviticus and Numbers are simply three of the five parts into which an originally longer work, the Torah, has been divided. These divisions are ancient; they were introduced many centuries before Christ. But they are not so ancient as the literary material itself; the purpose of these divisions, in this case as well, was likely to allow the entire work to be contained on scrolls of a more convenient size. (Within Judaism today a complete copy of the books of Moses is still often referred to as the "five fifths of the Torah.")

This long central section of the Torah, which begins when the Israelites leave Egypt and continues until they reach the borders of the land of Canaan, is structured by travel notices, for example, "The Israelites journeyed from Rameses to Sukkoth" (Exodus 12:37); "After leaving Sukkoth they camped at Etham on the edge of the desert" (Exodus 13:20). In between these notices are descriptions of what happened, whether much or little, at each place where the people stopped while on their journey. These descriptions actually constitute the highest-level literary units of which this section of the Torah is composed. But these units are of greatly varying length. Some are as short as a single sentence: "Then they came to Elim, where there were twelve springs and seventy palm trees, and they camped there near the water" (Exodus 15:27). But one unit, the so-called Sinai Pericope (the account of what happened while the Israelites were encamped before Mount Sinai), actually constitutes the vast bulk of this section, extending from Exodus 19:1 through Numbers 10:10. When viewed within this literary form, the "book" of Leviticus is recognized to be only part of one unit within one section of the Torah.

A case can nevertheless be made for treating Leviticus as a coherent whole. It describes its own content very accurately in its double concluding summaries: "These are the decrees, the laws and the regulations that the LORD established on Mount Sinai between himself and the Israelites through Moses" (Leviticus 26:46); "These are the commands the LORD gave Moses on Mount Sinai for the Israelites" (Leviticus 27:34). In other words, Leviticus is an ordered collection of the laws God gave Moses *while* the Israelites were at Mount Sinai. As such it can be meaningfully studied as a whole; as noted in Chapter One, I have elsewhere suggested at least one way in which it may be seen to have an elegant structure of its own.[5] But to understand the book within its literary context, we should additionally recognize the wider framework

---

5.   Christopher R. Smith, "The Literary Structure of Leviticus," *Journal for the Study of the Old Testament* 70 (1996): 17-32.

into which Leviticus has been set: it is only part of the Sinai Pericope, which itself is only part of the journey from Egypt to Canaan, which itself is one section of the Torah. We should not let traditional book boundaries and book names keep us from appreciating this setting.

But even as we seek to appreciate the Torah as a unified composition in order to understand its constituent parts within their broader literary context, there is also a sense in which we do need to see it as the "Pentateuch," or the "five books" of Moses. The division of the Torah into five parts is a tradition that was established so early that later biblical authors and editors echoed it in order to ascribe an authoritative character to their works. The division of Psalms into five "books," for example, coupled with the placement of a psalm at the head of the collection that encourages meditation on the "law of the LORD," seems intended to encourage the reading of this group of songs as "Scripture," just as one would read the Torah. Lamentations may similarly present five acrostic poems in order to allude to the Torah in some way. And at least according to one interpretation, Jesus may be depicted in Matthew as the "new Moses" by the way his teachings have been organized into five "books."[6]

Nevertheless, even though the tradition of a fivefold division has thus been "enscripturated" and can help inform our understanding of other books in the Bible, everything we have said about the value of approaching the Torah as a unified composition still holds. Tradition, in fact, testifies just as clearly to the unity of this work as to its division, for example, by the way the "books" into which it has been divided have always been known in Hebrew by their opening words, instead of by individual titles (as we will discuss further below).

So as we read Samuel-Kings, Chronicles-Ezra-Nehemiah and the Torah, we need to be aware of the ways that traditional book divisions can keep us from recognizing literary-structural patterns that run across more than one biblical "book." This, we have noted, is analogous to the

---

6.   A familiar example is B.W. Bacon, *Studies in Matthew* (New York: Holt, 1930).

way that chapter divisions can keep us from recognizing literary units within biblical books that are significantly larger than chapters.

But chapters can also misleadingly combine smaller separate units, and the same thing can happen in the case of book divisions. Specifically, the so-called "minor prophets" are sometimes treated as if they were a coherent literary unity, the "Book of the Twelve." In other words, the equivalent of a book boundary is often drawn around them, either formally, as when commentaries are written on this "Book of the Twelve," or informally, as when we group "all of those minor prophets" together in our thinking.

An effective book boundary around the minor prophets may actively undermine the essential meaning of the individual books that are being treated as smaller units within a larger literary whole. As Herbert Marks has observed,

> The final count of twelve prophets seems less a reflection of the material available than a deliberately imposed convention, designed to enforce a radical kind of closure. . . . In the Hebrew arrangement . . . the Twelve come immediately after the three "major" prophets, Isaiah, Jeremiah and Ezekiel. The pattern of three plus twelve recalls the three patriarchs and the twelve sons of Jacob—one of the basic paradigms of Israelite historiography . . . . By accommodating the prophetic corpus to such a type, the editors were in effect assimilating prophecy to a canonical rule, solidly rooted in communal tradition. . . . From this perspective, "The Book of the Twelve" may well be an anti-prophetic document, restricting prophecy to a limited number of sources, whose authority depends on established precedent.[7]

In other words, this is a case where a traditional book boundary (whether understood implicitly, through the idea of a "minor prophets" grouping, or more explicitly, if these writings are considered a single

---

7.   Herbert Marks, "The Twelve Prophets," *The Literary Guide to the Bible*, ed. Robert Alter and Frank Kermode (Cambridge, Mass: Harvard University Press, 1990), pp. 208-209.

"book") creates a "form" that not just obscures but actually undercuts the meaning of the writings it shapes. The twelve separate books known as the "minor prophets" should therefore not be combined into a "Book of the Twelve," any more than the pieces into which some longer books have been divided should be treated as whole works in their own right.

This is particularly the case since the tendency to treat these twelve prophetic works as if they were a single "book," a practice that admittedly has an ancient pedigree, can not be attributed to literary considerations—no overarching structural pattern ties them all together. Instead, it is likely due once again to scroll length: in this case, it was more convenient to copy several short books together onto a single scroll than to create a tiny scroll for each. But almost-mystical considerations also seem to have had an influence.

In the second century, Origen reported in his commentary on the Psalms that "the canonical books are twenty-two, according to the Hebrew tradition."[8] He then listed the books, showing how he arrived at this number, rather than the total of 39 we are used to today. Origen listed single books of Samuel and Kings, and of Chronicles and Ezra-Nehemiah, reflecting the first stage in the division of the two longer works we have just discussed, but not their subsequent division into four parts each. In Origen's list Joshua and Judges are combined, as are Jeremiah and Lamentations. And he apparently also considered the minor prophets a single "Book of the Twelve,"[9] yielding a total of 22 Old Testament books. Why this number? Origen argued that it was "not without reason" that the books of the Hebrew Bible were

---

8.   This fragment of the commentary is quoted in the *Philocalia*, chapter 3, "Why the Inspired Books are Twenty-two in Number," cited here in the translation by George Lewis (Edinburgh: T. & T. Clark, 1911), http://www.tertullian.org/fathers/origen_philocalia_02_text.htm#C3.

9.   Origen's list is found in another fragment from the Commentary on the Psalms quoted by Eusebius, *Church History*, VI.25.2. A "Book of the Twelve" is not actually listed, but can be inferred and is needed to arrive at a total of 22.

the same in number as the letters of the Hebrew alphabet. For as the twenty-two letters may be regarded as an introduction to the wisdom and the Divine doctrines given to men in those Characters, so the twenty-two inspired books are an alphabet of the wisdom of God and an introduction to the knowledge of realities.[10]

In other words, there should be 22 books in the Hebrew Scriptures because there were 22 letters in the Hebrew alphabet.

Jerome, who lived some two centuries later, arrived at the same total in much the same way, and for the same reason. (His list is identical to Origen's except that Ruth, rather than Joshua, is combined with Judges.) In his *Prologue to the Book of Kings* Jerome observed that "just as there are twenty-two elements [letters], by which we write in Hebrew all that we say, . . . thus twenty-two scrolls are counted, by which letters and writings a just man is instructed in the doctrine of God."[11] However, Jerome noted that others treated Ruth and Lamentations as distinct books, and thus reached a total of "twenty-four books of the Old Law." He observed that this was a figure that "the Apocalypse of John introduces with the number of twenty-four elders worshipping the Lamb and offering their crowns."[12] Thus book boundaries, and particularly the one around the "Twelve Prophets," were placed not by reference to literary-structural considerations, but rather in such a way as to reach totals with a mystical significance.

One other example of drawing book boundaries with numerical totals in mind is found in those churches in Syria, Egypt and Ethiopia that treat the final two collections of sayings in Proverbs as a separate book, the "Wisdom of Bagor" (that is, Agur).[13] It actually does make sense, on one level, not to include the sayings of Agur and Lemuel in a book

---

10.   *Philocalia*, chapter 3.

11.   Kevin P. Edgecomb, trans., "Jerome's 'Helmeted Introduction' to Kings," http://www.bombaxo.com/blog/?p=218.

12.   Ibid.

13.   Roger Beckwith, *The Old Testament Canon of the New Testament Church and Its Background in Early Judaism* (Grand Rapids: Eerdmans, 1985),p. 502, n. 17.

whose opening announces it to be "the proverbs of Solomon." However, even without these last two collections, that book still includes sayings by authors other than Solomon. Two anonymous groups of "sayings of the wise" intervene between the two collections of Solomon's proverbs. And the opening exhortations may not have been written by him either, since they are followed by the introductory heading "the proverbs of Solomon" as the sayings proper begin. The creation of a separate book from the last two collections in Proverbs may therefore have been motivated not so much by the wish to limit its sayings to those by Solomon as by an effort to create a "wisdom pentateuch." In the churches where the "Wisdom of Bagor" has been split off from Proverbs, the two resulting books are typically grouped together with Ecclesiastes, Ecclesiasticus and Wisdom of Solomon. In other words, as in the case of Psalms (and perhaps Lamentations and Matthew), the authoritative character of writings is being proclaimed by a fivefold division that reflects the traditional shape of the Torah. Even as we acknowledge the biblical wisdom books to be authoritative (although Protestants would hold that Ecclesiasticus and Wisdom of Solomon are deuterocanonical rather than fully canonical), it must still be insisted that book boundaries should not be determined by "Bible numerics" that invoke the numbers 5, 22 or 24, but rather by appeal to literary considerations by which distinct original compositions may be identified. And those considerations would suggest that Samuel-Kings, Chronicles-Ezra-Nehemiah, Luke-Acts, and each of the minor prophets be recognized as individual "books." They would also suggest that it is quite reasonable to leave the sayings of Agur and Lemuel in the multiple-author anthology in which they are most widely found.

BOOK SEQUENCE

The sequence in which we are accustomed to encountering the books of the Bible is a second traditional factor that can impede our understanding of the Scriptures.

For one thing, this sequence can obscure the *circumstances* under which books were composed. Consider, for example, the effects of the order in which we are now used to encountering Paul's letters. If we assign a number to each of his epistles based on a plausible understanding of when they were written (scholarly estimates would vary in certain cases), with the first being numbered "1," and so forth, we discover that the current arrangement presents them roughly in this sequence:

6, 3, 4, 5, 9, 10, 8, 1, 2, 11, 13, 12, 7.

This order actively discourages us from trying to understand Paul's letters as we should, within the context of his life and the development of his thought. Instead, we often encounter them more as rootless, ethereal documents, which is truly ironic, since so much in these letters is written to challenge and correct an other-wordly spirituality. The simple fact is that these epistles have been sorted into two groups (letters to churches and letters to individuals) and then arranged roughly by length, from longest to shortest, within each of these groups. This is no more helpful or meaningful an arrangement than the one a friend of mine encountered upon retuning home from college after a family move. He went up to his new room to discover that his mother had arranged his books on the shelves by color! So we should not grant this customary arrangement an authority that would allow its dehistoricizing effect on the Pauline corpus to continue unchecked. As G. C. D. Howley has noted,

> The arrangement of the letters of Paul in the New Testament is in general that of their length. When we rearrange them into their chronological order, fitting them as far as possible into their life-setting within the record of the Acts of the Apostles, they begin to yield up more of their treasure; they become self-explanatory, to a greater extent than when this background is ignored.[14]

The customary arrangement of the minor prophets similarly frustrates an attempt to understand these books within the context of the

---

14.   G.C.D. Howley, "The Letters of Paul," *New International Bible Commentary* (Grand Rapids: Zondervan, 1979), p. 1095.

prophetic tradition as it developed over the centuries. For example, for greatest understanding, we should read Amos, Hosea, Micah, and at least the beginning of Isaiah together, since they all speak to the same historical situation in the eighth century B.C. (J. B. Phillips encouraged just such a reading when he published his translations of these works in a single volume entitled *Four Prophets: Amos, Hosea, First Isaiah, Micah; A Modern Translation from the Hebrew*.)[15] But in the familiar order, Hosea is separated from Amos by the book of Joel, which could come from a much later time period. And Amos is separated from Micah by the book of Obadiah, which was written nearly 150 years later, and by the book of Jonah, which could also date from a much later period (even though it relates eighth-century events). On top of all this, the oracles of these three eighth-century "minor" prophets (Amos, Hosea and Micah) have been placed a great distance away, in a separate collection, from the oracles of Isaiah, who was their contemporary.

On what basis have the minor prophets been put in their traditional sequence? At least the first several books appear to have been ordered by catch-phrases:

"Return, Israel, to the LORD your God" (Hosea 14:1) connects with " 'Even now,' declares the LORD, 'return to me with all your heart' " (Joel 2:12).

"The LORD will roar from Zion and thunder from Jerusalem" (Joel 3:16) connects with "The LORD roars from Zion and thunders from Jerusalem" (Amos 1:2).

"So that they may possess the remnant of Edom and all the nations that bear my name" (Amos 9:12) connects with "People from the Negev will occupy the mountains of Esau, and people from the foothills will possess the land of the Philistines" (Obadiah 19).

This principle of organization moves readers of these books back and forth through time (very significantly, if Joel is as late a book as

---

15.   London: Geoffrey Bles and New York: Macmillan, 1963.

many scholars believe), and this discourages an appreciation of these prophetic oracles within their historical contexts.

The placement of books within the customary sequence can also create unjustified expectations about their *genre.* James has been placed at the head of the "general epistles," which are to all appearances a group of letters composed by leading figures of the church (also including Peter, John and Jude) and sent to wider audiences than Paul's epistles typically address. The book of James does begin like a letter, since it is intended to be read and heard by scattered believers throughout the Roman Empire. But after its opening, it does not follow the standard epistolary format of its day, which would ordinarily have included a thanksgiving and prayer, followed by the main body of the letter, and then some standard closing elements such as greetings. James instead offers just a mixture of short sayings and slightly longer discussions of practical subjects. While there is thematic continuity, there is not sequential development. In these ways the book of James actually has strong affinities with the wisdom literature of the Old Testament. A recognition of these affinities should inform our expectations as we read the book. But its placement encourages us to approach it with expectations that are appropriate for a letter instead.

We need to be equally careful about our expectations of genre as we read the book of Jonah. Jonah was a prophet, and the book of Jonah is a book about a prophet. But it is not a book of prophecy. That is, it is not a collection of poetic oracles, like most of the rest of the prophetic corpus, but rather a biographical narrative. There are also biographical narratives in some of the other prophetic books. In the story of Jonah, however, the prophet plays a symbolic role, emblematic of the nation of Israel, and for the purposes of this book, that role is actually more significant than his identity as a historical figure who brought the "word of the LORD" at a specific point in time. There are a few cases in which other prophets also played roles in which they symbolized the nation; Ezekiel was commanded to live on siege rations for over a year, for example, to announce the impending siege of Jerusalem (Ezekiel 4:9-17). But when other prophets performed signs or served as signs in this way, this was in obedience to God's commands. Jonah, however, serves as a sign because of his disobedience. (God didn't say to him, "Behold, I am sending you to Nineveh, but you shall flee to Tarshish instead, and when the people ask you, 'Why have you fled to Tarshish,' you shall say to them, 'Thus are you doing, O Israel . . .'") The reader of the book must make judgments throughout the story about what Jonah is doing, and why, and whether it is appropriate; in the end, the reader is actually meant to adopt an attitude opposite to Jonah's. In that sense, in its literary form at least, Jonah is actually is more like books in the wisdom tradition than those in the prophetic tradition, since it draws on the same analogical faculty that the parables and proverbs of wisdom writing do.

Jonah therefore represents something of a special case among the prophetic books, which typically consist of the oracles of an individual prophet, even if they also give some details about his life and in some cases include actual biographical narrative. Moreover, the other prophetic books appear to have been initially composed during or shortly after the prophet's lifetime, with a message to his contemporaries. The book of Jonah, on the other hand, may have been composed well after the prophet lived, with a message intended for a later generation in Israel. (Scholars who believe the book was written after Jonah's lifetime debate whether this was in an exilic or post-exilic setting.)

Despite all this, the essential message of the book of Jonah is about how the people can and must fulfill their unique role within God's purposes in salvation history. A good argument can therefore be made that the best place to locate this special case is still among the prophets, since that is their message as well. But readers should be aware of the particular challenges that the book of Jonah presents for interpretation. They should not let its placement in the midst of the prophetic corpus keep them from realizing that it is a different kind of writing from most of that corpus, and that they should engage it through an interpretive approach suited to its own genre.

In short, we should not uncritically embrace the expectations that the traditional sequence of the books of the Bible may create regarding a given book's circumstances of composition or literary genre. This is particularly true since the sequence we are familiar with reflects only the current state of a tradition that has varied from place to place and from time to time. Indeed, to have a fixed sequence at all is a more recent development. For the first three-quarters of the Bible's history, its books were presented in a great variety of orders.

Roger Beckwith notes that in the case of the Old Testament, "This stability of order is a relatively modern phenomenon, and owes a good deal to the invention of printing. It was preceded by an era of fluidity, both among the Jews (the chief guardians of the Hebrew Bible) and among Christians (the chief guardians of the Greek)."[16] Beckwith notes seventy-nine different attested orders for the books of the Old Testament. These orders were generated as various liturgical, historical and literary goals were pursued in the presentation of these books. There are some general constants: the "five books of Moses," for example, are nearly always kept together, as they should be, since they are they simply the parts into which the Torah has been divided. (In one case, however, the sequence is Genesis, Exodus, Leviticus, Joshua, Deuteronomy, Numbers.) Joshua, Judges, Samuel and Kings nearly always appear in this order (although in one case Jeremiah intervenes between Samuel and Kings, and Ruth is often attached to Judges). But

---

16. Beckwith, p. 181. It should be noted that Beckwith believes that the books of the Old Testament actually were in a fixed order in the time of Jesus. He thus considers the subsequent variations over the following centuries, in both Jewish and Christian versions of the Bible, a departure from this previously fixed order. Beckwith's overall goal is to establish that the *content* of the Old Testament canon was fixed by New Testament times. One argument he makes to this end is that the *order* of the canon was fixed by then. He supports this claim in various ways, but we do not need to consider his arguments here, since even if the Old Testament books were in a fixed order at the time of Jesus, Beckwith himself documents that their order became quite fluid right after the New Testament period. And it is precisely with the tradition that extends from after the New Testament period to the present that we are concerned. In terms of that tradition, a fixed book order truly is a "relatively modern phenomenon."

the other books of the Old Testament have been presented in many different sequences.

For the major prophets, the following orders are attested (with Lamentations sometimes appended to Jeremiah):

Isaiah-Jeremiah-Ezekiel

Isaiah-Ezekiel-Jeremiah

Jeremiah-Isaiah-Ezekiel

Jeremiah-Ezekiel-Isaiah

Ezekiel-Isaiah-Jeremiah

The minor prophets generally follow the major prophets in Hebrew manuscripts, but they precede them in many manuscripts of the Septuagint. And in the Septuagint the first six minor prophets appear in this order: Hosea, Amos, Micah, Joel, Obadiah, Jonah. The order that is customary in English Bibles is rather: Hosea, Joel, Amos, Obadiah, Jonah, Micah.

The group of Old Testament books known as the "Writings" appear in an even greater variety of orders than the prophets. In the tradition reflected in historic Christian Bibles, they are not even kept together consistently as a group. Job, for example, is put right after the Pentateuch in several cases. Chronicles can be placed after Samuel-Kings. Ruth, as we have already seen, is sometimes attached to Judges, and Lamentations can be appended to Jeremiah.

The books of the New Testament, for their part, also appear historically in a variety of orders. Bruce Metzger observes that these books are typically gathered into five groups, in this sequence: the gospels; Acts; Paul's epistles; the general (or "Catholic") epistles; and Revelation. But Metzger then notes, "Prior to the invention of printing, however, there were many other sequences, not only of the five main groups of books, but also of the several books within each group."[17] While the gospels, for example, are always kept together, they are found in nine different sequences, including two in which Luke is placed last and followed immediately by

17.   Bruce Metzger, *The Canon of the New Testament: Its Origin, Development, and Significance* (New York: Oxford University Press, 1987), p. 295.

Acts, possibly out of a desire to keep the two volumes of this historical study together. Acts usually follows the gospels, although in three cases the Pauline epistles intervene between the gospels and Acts, and Acts can also be found after both the Pauline and the general epistles.[18]

And while we are used to encountering Paul's letters before the general epistles, Metzger notes that "virtually all Greek manuscripts of the New Testament place the Catholic Epistles immediately after Acts and before the Pauline Epistles."[19] Paul's letters themselves appear in seventeen different sequences. Hebrews is typically placed at the end of them, but in various manuscripts it is instead inserted among them, in a number of different places: after Romans, 2 Corinthians, Galatians, or 2 Thessalonians. The general epistles, while always kept together according to authorship, nevertheless are found in seven different orders, including one that seems to be determined by the number of epistles each author wrote: John (3), Peter (2), Jude (1), James (1). A sequence in which the book of Revelation follows the gospels, instead of concluding the entire New Testament, is attested several times.[20]

Metzger concludes that "the very great variety in order, both of the several parts of the New Testament as well as of books within each part, leads one to conclude that such matters were of no great significance for the ancient and medieval Church; they became an issue only with later editors and publishers."[21] The advent of printing caused the order of the books of the Bible to become greatly standardized. Nevertheless, because of the way this order had already varied over time, at least four different "established" orders are now in use today: one by

---

18.   Kurt Aland and Barbara Aland, *The Text of the New Testament*, 2nd ed., trans. Erroll F. Rhodes (Grand Rapids: Eerdmans; Leiden: E.J. Brill, 1989), p. 79.

19.   Metzger, pp. 295-296.

20.   Richmond Lattimore revived this presentation in our day in the first volume of his New Testament translation, *The Four Gospels and the Revelation* (London: Hutchinson, 1980).

21.   Metzger, p. 300.

Protestants and Catholics;[22] one by Greek Orthodox Christians; one by Syrian Orthodox Christians; and one by Jews, for the Hebrew Scriptures. For that matter, as we will see in Chapter Three, various modern editions of the Bible have presented the books in other sequences. Any book order we might be familiar with and even take for granted, therefore, really only reflects the current state of a tradition that was fluid for much of its history and still varies today. This is all the more reason not to accept uncritically all of the interpretations that the book order we know today would suggest.

BOOK TITLES

The titles that have been assigned to the books of the Bible are a final factor that can interfere with our understanding of the Scriptures. While the biblical books bear titles that in many cases are very ancient, none of them are original. That is, they were not chosen by the authors, but rather assigned by tradition. Some of these titles have changed significantly over time, and even today certain books of the Bible are known by different titles in different places. In other words, like the customary book sequence, the list of book titles we are familiar with simply represents the current shape of a fluid tradition.

In the Hebrew Bible, titles were typically given to individual books that either referred to their authors or main characters (e.g. Jeremiah, Ruth), or else were descriptive of their content (Psalms, for example, was called *Tehillim*, "praises"). But the Torah was treated differently. It was customarily divided into five books, and their opening words were used as their titles. The book we know as Genesis, for example, was called *Bereshith*, "In the Beginning." Exodus was referred to as *Shemoth*, "Names," since

---

22. Catholic Bibles additionally contain the deuterocanonical or apocryphal books, interspersed among the fully canonical books.

this book begins, "These are the names of the sons of Israel who went to Egypt with Jacob." And so forth.[23]

Some of these first-line titles actually seem to have been shortened over the years. In his commentary on Psalms (around A.D. 240), Origen wrote that the Jews of his day called Exodus *Welesmoth*.[24] This was an abbreviation of *w'elleh shemoth*, "These are the names," but a longer one than *Shemoth*, the name that Jews use for this book today. Origen also notes that Deuteronomy was called *Eleaddebareim*, from the book's opening *eleh haddebarim*, "These are the words Moses spoke to all Israel." Jews now call this book simply *Debarim*, "words."

When the Old Testament was translated into Greek in the few centuries before the start of our era, its books were given titles that were, for the most part, simply translations into Greek of their traditional Hebrew titles. *Shoftim*, for example, became *Kritai*; both words mean "Judges." *Qoholeth*, "preacher," became *Ecclesiastes*. When the Hebrew titles were proper names, Greek forms were used, so that *Tsephanyah* (Zephaniah) became *Sophonias*. But in some cases the titles were actually changed. The five books of the Torah were no longer described by their opening words, but given Greek titles that were intended to reflect their content. *Bereshith* thus became *Genesis* ("beginning" or "origin"), *Shemoth* became *Exodus* ("going out"), and so on. There seems to have been variety in some of these names before they became standardized; *Exodus* was also called *Exagoge* ("leading out") and *Deuteronomy* ("second law") was also known as *Epinomis* ("after-law") and as the *Protreptika* or the *Paraineseis* ("exhortations"). Judges was also called "Judgements," and Psalms was sometimes known as "Hymns."[25]

---

23.   Mary Douglas carried this Hebrew convention over into English when she chose, as the title for her commentary on the book of Numbers, *In the Wilderness* (Sheffield, England: Sheffield Academic Press, 1993).

24.   Quoted by Eusebius, *Church History*, VI.25.2

25.   These names are attested by Philo and the Hellenist Ezekiel in Alexandria (Beckwith, p. 246).

The names of some other books were also changed when they were translated into Greek, even though they were already known by specific titles, rather than by their first lines. These new Greek names reflected a different understanding of their content from the one suggested by their Hebrew titles. The Jews called the book of Chronicles, for example, *Dibre ha-yomim*, literally "words of the days," describing a regularly-kept record of events. But in Greek this book was retitled *Paralipomenon*, meaning "things left aside," "leftovers," or "omissions." This was a reference to the significant amount of material the book contained that was not in the history of the same events narrated in Samuel and Kings. And those books, for their part, were each retitled *Basileion*: "Kingdoms" or, perhaps more accurately (based on what we have already observed about how this extended work is structured), "Reigns." (As we noted above, these works were divided when they were translated, resulting in a First and Second *Paralipomenon* and First through Fourth Reigns.)

The New Testament books, for their part, were also not named by their authors. They, too, were given traditional titles as they were collected into the scriptural canon. Most of the New Testament books are letters, and these were named after either their authors or their recipients. The gospels were named after their presumed authors, while the *Praxeis Apostolon* (Acts of the Apostles) was named after its main characters and the *Apocalypsis Ioannou* (Revelation of John) after its recipient and author.

Some further changes to the titles of the biblical books were made in the Vulgate, Jerome's influential translation of the Bible into Latin, which he completed near the end of the fourth century. For the most part Jerome adopted the traditional Greek titles and simply translated them, so that *Arithmoi* became *Numeri*, "Numbers"; *Kritai* became the *Liber Iudicum*, "Book of Judges"; and *Paroimiai* became *Liber Proverbiorum*, "Book of Proverbs." Proper names that functioned as book titles appeared in Latinized forms in the Vulgate. But instead of translating the titles of some books, Jerome transliterated them. That is, he carried them over letter-for-letter from the Greek. Transliterated titles included Genesis, Exodus, Leviticus, Deuteronomy, Psalms, Ecclesiastes and *Para-*

lipomenon. Finally, aware that the books that were known in Greek as First through Fourth Reigns had originally been entitled Samuel and Kings in Hebrew, Jerome provided a double name for each of these books. He used the term "Kings" instead of "Reigns," and so called the first two books both 1-2 Samuel and 1-2 Kings, and the next two both 1-2 Kings and 3-4 Kings.

Finally, when the Bible was translated into the vernacular languages of Europe, most of these titles from the Latin version were adopted. Typically this was through translation (so that *Canticum canticorum,* for example, became the Song of Songs in English). But sometimes it was once again through transliteration, so that Greek titles like Genesis and Ecclesiastes found their way from Greek through Latin into English and other languages. And one of the books had its title changed back to something closer in meaning to its traditional Hebrew title. Martin Luther was aware that while the Greek title *Paralipomenon* had been retained in the Vulgate, Jerome had also commented that the book could be called "more clearly a *chronicle* of all of Divine history."[26] Luther adopted this suggestion, using the name *die Chronika* in his German Bible. His example was soon followed in other European languages. Hence we today know this book, in the two parts into which it was divided, as First and Second Chronicles, under the "new" name it was given during the Reformation after going by *Paralipomenon* in Greek and Latin Bibles for well over 1500 years.

Luther also changed some other titles. Rather than continue to transliterate the Greek word *Ecclesiastes* as Jerome had done, he translated the Hebrew *Qoholeth* as *Prediger* ("Preacher"). Rather than offer a word-for-word translation of the Hebrew title *Shir ha-Shirim* ("Song of Songs"), he translated the meaning of the phrase, entitling this book the *Hohelied* or "High Song," meaning the "best song." And

---

26.   Kevin P. Edgecomb, trans., "Jerome's 'Helmeted Introduction' to Kings," http://www.bombaxo.com/blog/?p=218 (emphasis added).

he called the Acts of the Apostles the *Apostelgeschichte,* or "history of the apostles."

The various biblical books have therefore experienced a number of different kinds of title changes over the centuries. The ones that have changed the least are those whose titles are based on proper names. But even these have altered in form as they have moved from one language to another (from *Tsephanyah* to *Sophonias* to Zephaniah, for example). Other titles have changed more significantly. Books that were originally known by their first lines in Hebrew (the books of the Pentateuch, and Lamentations) were given Greek titles that described their contents instead. And some titles that already were descriptive were changed to reflect a different understanding of a book's contents. Finally, the titles of some books were transliterated instead of being translated; as a result, they ceased to be a meaningful description of the book in the new language and became simply a proper name. Some books have actually undergone two or more of these kinds of changes. Deuteronomy, for example, was originally known by its first line in Hebrew; it was then given a content-descriptive title in Greek, but now it is known by a trans- literation of that title that basically functions as a proper name.

Even now some biblical books are known by different titles in different contexts. The King James Version follows Jerome's example of giving two different names for the books into which Samuel and Kings were divided, referring, for instance, to "The First Book of Samuel, Otherwise Called, the First Book of the Kings." Song of Songs is known in many English versions as Song of Solomon. (Modern Bible publishers have also felt a certain liberty to rename books, as we will see in more detail in our next chapter.)

In light of this survey, it should be clear that the biblical book titles we are familiar with simply reflect the current state of a fluid tradition. In their case the tradition is admittedly less fluid than in the case of book order. Book order varied significantly until the invention of printing in the fifteenth century, while the book titles we know are essentially derived from the fourth-century Vulgate (although for English Bibles, Anglo-Saxon terms were used in place of Latin ones in some cases, and

Paralipomenon became Chronicles). Despite this essential continuity for so many centuries, we must recognize that these book titles are not necessarily a reliable indication of content or message.

How is our understanding of the books of the Bible affected by their traditional titles? Let us consider, to begin with, the matter of *authorship*. It is evident that the tradition has had a tendency to attribute anonymous books to known figures. None of the five songs in the book of Lamentations, for example, are ascribed to anyone. In Greek translation, however, this book was given the title "The Lamentations of Jeremiah," and the association of the book with that prophet continues to this day. Its traditional placement right after Jeremiah reinforces this association. (Lamentations has sometimes even been attached to that prophetic work.) The attribution to Jeremiah may derive from the report that he "composed laments for Josiah" after that king was killed in battle (2 Chronicles 35:25). It is certainly plausible that Jeremiah might also have written laments twenty-three years later, when Jerusalem was destroyed. But in our interpretation of the book of Lamentations, we need to be open to the possibility that its songs were actually written by one or more persons other than Jeremiah, at some time other than when he lived.

To cite another example, there is no specific claim of authorship within the pages of the "Gospel of Matthew," either. Thus, there is no scriptural authority to assign it to the disciple Matthew; this title actually comes from tradition. Nevertheless, if we allow ourselves to be guided by this tradition, we will be likely to read this work as if it were a first-generation Christian document, since it would have been written by a companion of Jesus. But it is possible that second-generation concerns actually motivated its anonymous author, and so we cannot let the traditional title keep us from appreciating that possibility.

Some editions of the Bible actually elaborate on the traditional book names and assign even more books to well-known figures. For example, the King James Version speaks of "The Epistle of Paul the Apostle to the Hebrews." But if we truly want to understand this book, we should not begin with the assumption that Paul wrote it. We must observe, for example, that it is the work of an author who considers himself to have heard about Jesus from others (Hebrews 2:3), while Paul insisted that he had met Jesus personally (1 Corinthians 9:1). It is written to Jewish believers to argue that a new covenant has replaced the old one (Hebrews 8:13), while Paul characteristically spoke more appreciatively of the old covenant, as containing promises through which the Gentiles could be included with the Jews (e.g. Galatians 3:17-29). For Paul the "true temple" is the Christian community, in which God now dwells by the Spirit, while for the author of Hebrews, the "true temple" is the heavenly one that served as a model for the earthly tabernacle (Hebrews 8:5). In short, while the emphases of Hebrews are not contradictory to Paul's, they are complementary, and so they must not be simply assimilated to his on the basis of a traditional authorship assumption.

The King James Version speaks similarly of "The Revelation of St. John the Divine," directly attributing this book to the same author as the Gospel of John. But we should not let this attribution keep us from recognizing that Revelation comes from a stream within early Christianity quite different from the one in which that gospel was written, making it improbable that a single person was responsible for both books. Indeed, the fact that the author of Revelation identifies himself as "John" actually suggests that he was not the same person responsible for the Gospel of John. That book's author does not write in his own name, but identifies himself only as "the disciple whom Jesus loved." It may still be inferred reasonably from the text of this gospel that its author was the apostle John; but if he did not wish to name himself there, why would he have named himself in the book of Revelation? It seems even more unlikely that he would have done so when we consider that in his second and third epistles, he calls himself simply "the elder," while in his first epistle, the sender's name is not provided at all.

So we should not consider the traditional titles to provide a reliable indication of a book's *author* in every case. We should also be careful not to allow these titles to encourage debatable assumptions about the *intended audience* or recipients of a biblical book. The book of Ephesians, in the form we know it today, is addressed to "God's holy people in

Ephesus." However, the phrase "in Ephesus" is not found in several early and important witnesses, and so this phrase, on which the book's traditional title is based, may be a later addition. There are suggestions within the epistle itself that Paul is writing to a group of believers he has never met: he tells them that he has "heard about" their faith (1:15), and says later that they have no doubt "heard about" him as well (3:2). He would hardly write this to the Ephesians, among whom he lived for two years. Nor does Paul include any greetings in this letter, as he likely would have if he were writing to his old friends in Ephesus. And so this may instead be either the letter to the Laodiceans mentioned at the end of Colossians, or else a circular letter sent to a group of churches in Asia Minor.

The traditional titles can also mislead us with regard to a book's *central focus*. We saw earlier that the name Genesis is derived from a Greek word meaning "beginnings" or "origins." This name might lead us to believe that the purpose of the book of Genesis is to tell us how everything got here. But this book is really much more about the series of covenants God inaugurated for his dealings with humanity than it is about the physical origins of the universe. But we may be looking with such interest throughout the book for the "how" of origins that we miss this covenantal emphasis entirely.

In the same way, we would expect a book with a title of "Exodus" to describe a group's departure from a place, and this book indeed describes how the Israelites came forth from Egypt. But it has much more to say about the covenant at Sinai and the construction of the tabernacle than about this "exodus." Given its title, however, we might be tempted to consider ourselves finished with the book's "main business" after we have read only the first third of it.

Book titles can also lead us to have the wrong expectations of a book's *genre*. The book of James begins as a letter would, and so it is customarily entitled "the epistle of James." However, as we noted above, this book actually has very strong affinities to works of wisdom literature such as Proverbs. It presents a series of pithy sayings and brief reflections on the human condition. It does not develop logically and systematically, the way an epistle would. And so we should not seek to understand this book as if it were an ordinary "epistle."

We may thus conclude that the familiar titles of the biblical books are yet another traditional factor that can interfere with our understanding of Scripture. These titles can misrepresent the contents and emphases of books, as well as encourage debatable assumptions about their authors, audience and genre. We should therefore not be guided by these titles any more than we should uncritically embrace the expectations that the traditional book sequence might create about genre or circumstances of composition, or the understanding that the traditional book divisions would encourage of literary unities in the Bible.

CONCLUSION

We still ought to approach the Bible on the book level. But we do need to be aware of how the boundaries, sequence, and titles to which we are accustomed can keep us from engaging the biblical books on their own terms. None of these are original, and the sequence and titles in particular simply reflect the current state of a tradition that has varied significantly over time, and which still varies from place to place today. We should therefore not allow these elements to continue governing our interpretations to the extent that they currently do. In our approach to the Bible, we must rather be careful to be informed and guided not by such traditional elements, but by the structures and emphases inherent in the biblical books themselves.

In our next chapter, we will consider how the Bible has been presented, in English editions since the early 1700s, in such a way as to de-emphasize the traditional factors we have been considering that can create so much difficulty for us as we read and seek to understand the books of the Bible.

3

Non-Traditional English Bibles

John Locke (1632-1704) is recognized as "one of the greatest thinkers of the early modern era." His "epistemological, linguistic, philosophical and political ideas have had a profound influence" that "still continues today."[1] Nevertheless, despite all of his brilliance, Locke admitted that he found it difficult to understand Paul's epistles. He eventually concluded that much of the problem lay in how he was reading them.

Locke had been following a typical practice of his time, which is still common today: he would read only one chapter of the Bible at a sitting, and if he came across any "hard places," he would "consult expositors" to try to find out what they meant.[2] But this, he finally realized, "was not a right method to get into the true sense of these epistles":

---

1.   Library of the University of Amsterdam, "Electronic edition of John Locke's drafts for the *Essay Concerning Human Understanding*," http://www.uba.uva.nl/digital_production_centre.

2.   John Locke, "An Essay for the Understanding of St. Paul's Epistles, by Consulting St. Paul Himself," *The Works of John Locke*, 12th ed. (London: Rivington et al., 1824), 7:xiii. (Facsimile edition, http://oll.libertyfund.org/Home3/Book.php?recordID=0128.07)

I saw plainly, after I began once to reflect on it, that if any one now should write me a letter, as long as St. Paul's to the Romans, . . . if I should divide it into fifteen or sixteen chapters, and read of them one to-day, and another to-morrow . . . I should never come to a full and clear comprehension of it. The way to understand the mind of him that [wrote] it, every one would agree, was to read the whole letter through, from one end to the other, all at once, to see what was the main subject and tendency of it: or if it had several views and purposes in it . . . to discover what those different matters were, and where the author concluded one, and began another; and if there were any necessity of dividing the epistle into parts, to make these the boundaries of them.[3]

Unfortunately, Locke observed, not only had Paul's letters been divided into chapters, which discouraged people from reading them all the way through, those divisions had not been logically placed. "The chapters the apostle's epistles are divided into," he lamented, "do end sometimes in the middle of a discourse, and sometimes in the middle of a sentence."[4] Even worse, because smaller verse divisions had also been incorporated into the text, Paul's letters were

so chopped and minced, and, as they are now printed, stand so broken and divided, that not only the common people take the verses usually for distinct aphorisms; but even men of more advanced knowledge, in reading them lose very much of the strength and force of the coherence, and the light that depends on it.[5]

Locke therefore decided that in order to understand Paul's epistles, he would have to read them in a new way.

I concluded it necessary, for the understanding of any one of St. Paul's epistles, to read it all through at one sitting; and to observe, as well as I could, the drift and design of his writing it. If the first reading

---

3.   Ibid.
4.   Ibid., p. vii.
5.   Ibid, vi-vii.

gave me some light, the second gave me more; and so I persisted on, reading constantly the whole epistle over at once, till I came to have a good general view of the apostle's main purpose in writing the epistle, the chief branches of his discourse wherein he prosecuted it, the arguments he used, and the disposition of the whole. This, I confess, is not to be obtained by one or two hasty readings; it must be repeated again and again, with a close attention to the tenour of the discourse, and *a perfect neglect of the divisions into chapters and verses.*[6]

Locke realized that putting Paul's letters into a different format would help him make the necessary change in his reading habits. And so he prepared manuscripts of five epistles (Romans, 1 Corinthians, 2 Corinthians, Galatians and Ephesians) in which they were no longer "chopped and minced" into chapters and verses. He put the text of the King James Version at the top of the page; it appeared, as was customary, one paragraph per verse, as if they were each indeed a "distinct aphorism." But below this text Locke wrote out his own paraphrase of the epistle, printed continuously in a single column, with paragraph divisions placed only where he felt there were natural breaks. He moved all of the verse numbers to the left margin, and placed chapter numbers at the top of the page.

Locke prepared these manuscripts initially for his own private use, but when he showed them to some friends, they urged him to have them published. As he himself explained,

[S]ome very sober, judicious Christians, no strangers to the sacred scriptures, nay, learned divines of the church of England, . . . professed, that by the perusal of these following papers, they understood the epistles much better than they did before, and . . . with repeated instances, pressed me to publish them."[7]

---

6.   Ibid., p. xiii (emphasis added).

7.   Ibid., p. xii.

Locke's health was by this time seriously declining, but he left instructions before his death in 1704 that his work on these epistles was to be made public. His paraphrases and notes were published in five separate volumes starting in 1705, and the whole collection was printed together in 1707. An essay by Locke on "Understanding Paul's Epistles by Consulting St. Paul Himself" was included as the introduction.[8] Thus it was that only about 150 years after verse divisions were first incorporated into the text of Scripture, at least one intelligent reader was already calling for them, and the chapter divisions, to be taken out.

James Peirce, a Nonconformist minister in Exeter, was inspired by Locke's example and began to prepare paraphrases of other epistles. He finished Colossians, Ephesians and most of Hebrews before he unfortunately passed away himself. Thus the promising possibility that a New Testament with marginalized verse numbers might be created in the Eighteenth Century was ultimately not realized.[9]

Nevertheless, Locke was the first of many English-language editors and publishers who sought to mute or eliminate the traditional elements that can make it so difficult for readers to understand and enjoy the Bible. Their work provided precedents and inspiration for us in the Bible Design Group (whose story I will tell in Chapter Four). As we began our task, we were aware of several of the editions discussed in this chapter; as our work progressed, we learned of others. These Bibles, testaments and portions suggested useful approaches to us; in some cases, they confirmed directions we were already taking. Considered as a group, they provide further evidence of the way traditional elements in the Bible interfere with understanding and enjoyment, in that they show how greatly the experience of reading can be improved when these elements are eliminated. In this chapter we will revisit each of the traditional

---

8.   John Locke, *A paraphrase and notes on the Epistles of St. Paul to the Galatians, I & II Corinthians, Romans, Ephesians* (London: Awnsham and John Churchill, 1707).

9.   See James Peirce, *A paraphrase and notes on the Epistles of St. Paul to the Colossians, Philippians, and Hebrews: after the manner of Mr. Locke* (London: J. Noon and J. Chandler, 1727).

factors we discussed in Chapters One and Two and consider the ways in which publishers have tried to help readers overcome their influence.

(I have not had the opportunity to investigate in detail whether publishers in languages other than English have made similar efforts, but I would not be surprised if they had. *The Jerusalem Bible*, discussed below, is actually a translation of *La Bible de Jérusalem*,[10] which appears in its standard editions in a single column with marginalized chapter and verse numbers. So at least one French edition has taken some of the measures discussed in this chapter. Moreover, at the start of the last century, Hermann von Soden wrote in his monumental text-critical work *Die Schriften des Neuen Testaments:*

> It is high time, in any editions that wish to facilitate rather than impede readers' understanding of the New Testament writings, for not only the verse divisions . . . but also the conventional chapter divisions to disappear completely from the text and to placed as inconspicuously as possible in the margins. Without giving any consideration to these divisions, the text must be printed in a way that will illustrate visually what units the authors themselves created within their works.[11]

It would be interesting to discover whether any German publishers have heeded this call.)

---

10.   École Biblique de Jérusalem, *La Bible de Jérusalem* (Paris: Desclée de Brouwer, 1961).

11.   "Und darum ist es hoch an der Zeit, dass in allen Textausgaben, wollen sie dem Leser das Verständnis der neut. Schriften erleichtern und nich erschweren, nicht nur die . . . Verseinteiung, sondern ganz ebenso die übliche Kapiteleinteilung aus dem Textbild völlig verschwinde und möglichst unauffällig am Rand angebracht werde. Der Text muss ohne jede Rücksicht darauf in einer Weise gedruckt werden, welche die vom Verfasser selbst seiner Schrift gegebene Gliederung zur Anschauung bringt." Hermann von Soden, *Die Schriften des Neuen Testaments* (Goettingen: Vandenhoeck and Ruprecht, 1911), I:482.

CHAPTERS AND VERSES

While a presentation of the Scriptures with chapter and verse numbers inserted into the text remains the standard format, editions without inserted numbers have appeared so frequently that they cannot be considered unusual. Indeed, J. Carter Swaim could observe matter-of-factly in 1953, "The Bible in our time has been issued in many different formats. It has appeared in two-column pages and one-column pages . . . with verse numbers and without."[12] A range of approaches have been taken, from placing all chapter and verse numbers in the margin, to representing them there only selectively, to removing them from the page entirely. The publishers of these editions often stated explicitly that their goal in taking verses out of the text was to promote reading with greater understanding and enjoyment.

In 1923, for example, the University of Chicago released *The New Testament: An American Translation* by Edgar J. Goodspeed, an edition in which all chapter and verse numbers were moved to the margins. In his introduction, Goodspeed wrote that he had wanted to "bring home the great, living messages of the New Testament a little more widely and forcibly to the life of our time." He therefore acknowledged the "generous co-operation of the University Press" that had "made it possible to print the translation as one would a modern book . . . and so facilitate reading, reference and understanding."[13] *The Old Testament: An American Translation* followed four years later. Lead translator J. M. Powis Smith explained in his own introduction, "The translators and the University Press have sought to give this work the appearance of a modern book. This purpose has . . . kept the verse numbers out of the text and relegated them to the margin, so that the reading of the text may not be inter-

---

12.   J. Carter Swaim, *Right and Wrong Ways to Use the Bible* (Philadelphia: Westminster Press, 1953), p. 7.

13.   Edgar J. Goodspeed, Preface to *The New Testament: An American Translation*, reprinted in *The Complete Bible: An American Translation* (Chicago: University Press, 1939), p. iv (N.T.).

rupted."[14] In this "Smith-Goodspeed" Bible (as *An American Translation* became known when the two testaments were published together), the marginal verse numbers are of a smaller size, and the chapter numbers appear in slightly larger, bold type.

Other editions took the same approach, but made the Bible look even more like a "modern book" by presenting the text in a single column, instead of the two columns that the Smith-Goodspeed Bible (and some other editions that also marginalized the numbers[15]) retained from the customary format. Among these were *The Twentieth Century New Testament* (1901), *The New Testament in Modern Speech* by Francis Weymouth (1903), Charles Cutler Torrey's *The Four Gospels: A New Translation* (1933), William Beck's *The New Testament in the Language of Today* (1963), *The Jerusalem Bible* (1966) and *The New English Bible* (1970).[16] The publishers of this last edition explained in a note that the numbers had been moved to the margins because the "conventional verse divisions in the New Testament date only from 1551 and have no basis in the manuscripts," adding that "[a]ny system of division into numbered verses is foreign to the spirit of this translation, which is intended to convey the meaning in continuous natural English."[17]

---

14.   J. M. Powis Smith, Preface to *The Old Testament: An American Translation*, reprinted in *The Complete Bible*, p. xv (O.T.).

15.   Including, for example, James Moffatt's widely-circulated *The New Testament: A New Translation* (New York: George Doran and London: Hodder and Stoughton, 1913).

16.   *The Twentieth Century New Testament* (London: Horace Marshall & Son and New York & Chicago: Fleming H. Revell, 1901); Francis Weymouth, *The New Testament in Modern Speech* (London: James Clarke and Co., 1903); Charles Cutler Torrey, *The Four Gospels: A New Translation*, 2nd ed. (New York and London: Harper and Brothers, 1947); William F. Beck, *The New Testament in the Language of Today* (St. Louis: Concordia, 1963); *The Jerusalem Bible* (Garden City, New York: Doubleday, 1966); *The New English Bible with Apocrypha* (New York: Oxford University Press, 1970).

17.   *The New English Bible*, pp. ix (N.T.). A similar explanation was offered for the Old Testament, p. xxi (O.T.).

Other publishers went even further. Some continued to put all the chapter numbers in the margins, but indicated only selected verse numbers there. For example, Richard Moulton, who (as we saw in Chapter One) complained in his introduction to *The Modern Reader's Bible* of 1907 that "when we open our ordinary versions . . . the eye catches nothing but a monotonous uniformity of numbered sentences, more suggestive of an itemised legal instrument than of what we understand as literature,"[18] put only a handful of verse numbers in the margin of each page. In *The Original New Testament* (1985), Hugh Schonfield marked only every fifth verse. He explained, "There were no chapters and verses in the manuscripts. The chapters now in use were adopted in the thirteenth century and the verse divisions as late as the sixteenth century. Their value was to assist in reading and reference, but they are in no sense authoritative."[19]

Other editions provided even fewer references—only one for each paragraph. Alexander Campbell published an edition of the New Testament in 1826 entitled *The Sacred Writings* (also known as *The Living Oracles*). He took up George Campbell's 1778 translation of the gospels and James MacKnight's 1795 translation of the epistles, supplemented these with the books of Acts and Revelation from Philip Doddridge's 1765 New Testament, and amended the whole text by reference to Griesbach's 1805 Greek critical apparatus. But Campbell paid careful attention not just to translation and textual criticism, but also to presentation. He recognized that as much of the original meaning of the Bible could be lost through defects in presentation as through archaic terminology or reliance on inferior manuscripts. Campbell lamented the effects of "cutting up the sacred text into morsels, called verses." "Many passages, otherwise plain and forcible," he noted, "have

---

18.   Richard Moulton, "Preface," *The Modern Reader's Bible* (New York: Macmillan, 1907), p. v.

19.   Hugh J. Schonfield, "Preface," *The Original New Testament* (San Francisco: Harper and Row, 1985), p. xxxi.

been weakened and obscured by this absurd interference."[20] Campbell would therefore not have included chapter or verse numbers anywhere, except that he wanted readers to have the option of "comparing any sentence . . . with the common version" (meaning the King James), and he felt that some notations were therefore necessary. "To checker the margin with a column of figures marking every verse in the common version, appeared no way profitable to the reader," he explained. "It rather perplexes the eye and distracts the attention of the reader, as well as dislocates the sense, and perpetuates what ought soon to be forgotten."[21] But he did include sparse notations at the head of each paragraph: a Roman numeral if a chapter began there, an Arabic verse number if one did not, and both if a new chapter had begun within the body of the preceding paragraph (e.g. "XI. 2." at the start of Paul's discussion of head coverings in First Corinthians). Over a century later, J. B. Phillips would present his *New Testament in Modern English* in essentially the same format, except that he included both a chapter and a verse number at the start of each paragraph.

Many of today's readers will be familiar with *The Message*, Eugene Peterson's paraphrase of the Scriptures,[22] and know that there were originally no verse numbers on its pages at all. Boldface chapter numbers two lines high still appeared in left-margin inserts, and a chapter-and-verse range for each page was provided at the top, but otherwise the text and margins were clear and clean, making *The Message* in its original form eminently readable. (A later "remix" edition put verse numbers

---

20. Alexander Campbell, "Preface to the Epistles," *The Sacred Writings of the Apostles and Evangelists of Jesus Christ, Commonly Styled, The New Testament* (1826); reprinted as *The Living Oracles* (Nashville: Gospel Advocate Restoration Reprints, 2001), p. xxx.

21. Campbell, "General Preface." These statements are made in one of several paragraphs not found in the Nashville reprint, but included in the transcription of Campbell's preface at http://www.mun.ca/rels/restmov/oracles1st/preface.html.

22. Eugene H. Peterson, *The Message: The Bible in Contemporary Language* (Colorado Springs: NavPress, 2002).

back in the margins.[23]) Around the same time that the New Testament in Peterson's paraphrase was first published, another edition that presented chapter numbers but not verse numbers was also issued, *The Unvarnished New Testament*, translated by Andy Gaus.[24] In this edition chapter numbers, similarly in large type, were centered on the page.

Still other editions removed chapter and verse numbers from the margin entirely. In Richmond Lattimore's translation of the New Testament, only a chapter and verse range for the whole page was provided, in the format COLOSSIANS: 2.11|3.1, in a header separated from the text by a horizontal line.[25]

But the logical extreme in muting this traditional factor was reached by *The Bible Designed to be Read as Living Literature* of 1936, in which no chapter or verse numbers were indicated anywhere on the page, not even in a range. Its editor, Ernest Sutherland Bates, lamented the difficulties that the customary presentation created for readers of the Bible:

> Certainly, no literary format was ever less conducive to pleasure or understanding than is the curious and complicated panoply in which the Scriptures have come down to us. None but a work of transcendent literary genius could have survived such a handicap at all. . . . [A]ll the poetry is printed as prose; while all the long paragraphs of prose are broken up into short verses, so that they resemble the little passages set our for parsing or analysis in an examination paper.[26]

---

23.   Eugene H. Peterson, *The Message//Remix: The Bible in Contemporary Language* (Colorado Springs: NavPress, 2005).

24.   Andy Gaus, trans., *The Unvarnished New Testament* (Grand Rapids: Phanes Press, 1991).

25.   Richmond Lattimore, *The New Testament* (New York: North Point Press, 1996). This volume combines Lattimore's *The Four Gospels and the Revelation* (New York: Farrar, Strauss, Giroux, 1979) and *Acts and Letters of the Apostles* (New York: Farrar, Strauss, Giroux, 1982).

26.   Ernest Sutherland Bates, "The Bible as Literature," *The Bible Designed to Be Read as Living Literature* (New York: Simon and Schuster, 1936), p. viii-ix. The final sentence is actually a quotation from an essay by Arthur Quiller-Couch, describing how a format similar to the Bible's would impair readers' understanding of an anthology

It was precisely to help free the Scriptures from this "handicap" that Bates eliminated numbering entirely. This move, together with ample margins, a single-column format, and a beautiful 14-point font designed by Frederic W. Goudy, gave *The Bible Designed to be Read as Living Literature* a fresh, clean, inviting appearance. It was a Bible that could be read with perhaps more pleasure and understanding than many had ever experienced before in their engagement with the Scriptures. Readers responded enthusiastically. Bates's edition became a bestseller; it was offered as a Book of the Month Club selection, remained in print for over 20 years and was reissued by the original publisher in 1993, with Lodowick Allison as its new editor.

The only drawback, and it was a very unfortunate one, was that this edition was a severe abridgment of the Bible. I would argue, in fact, that even though the presentation made the Scriptures very appealing on the visual level, Bates' extensive deletions rendered the Scriptures far worse as literature, and therefore made them much less enjoyable and understandable on the literary level. (To cite just one example, Bates systematically eliminated all but one of the occurrences of the "generations" formula in the book of Genesis. In several cases, in fact, he deleted only the "generations" formula while retaining all of the surrounding text. But most interpreters agree that readers are meant to rely on this formula to guide them through this book's 12-part structure. Bates' Genesis is still a collection of interesting stories, but without any overarching shape or order.[27]) Nevertheless, *The Bible*

---

of English literature. But the reference is indirectly to customary format of the Bible itself.

27.   As one reviewer of the edition observed when it was re-issued, "[R]ecent scholarship has argued that those genealogies that Bates found so expendable actually serve as major structuring elements in books such as Genesis and Numbers. Without them, the narratives, upon which Bates places such stress, seem disconnected . . . and the reader inevitably misses the unity of these books and other larger textual units." Jon D. Levenson, "Review of *The Bible Designed to be Read as Living Literature*," *National Review*, Nov. 15, 1993, http://findarticles.com/p/articles/mi_m1282/is_n22_v45/ai_14667476.

Designed to Be Read as Living Literature remains an inspiring example of how appealingly the Scriptures can be presented. In fact, one of our goals in producing *The Books of The Bible* was to put the entire Scriptures, unabridged, in as appealing a format as Bates had used for the portions he selected for his volume.

Numerous editors and publishers, therefore, aware of the ways that chapters and verses can obscure form and meaning in the Bible, have used a variety of approaches to diminish their appearance and minimize their effects. But this is actually only half the battle. It is also a great service to readers to help them become aware of the literary structures that chapters and verses typically disguise. Many of the publications just mentioned used various means to highlight these structures, as they were reasonably understood by the translators and editors.

REPRESENTATION OF THE LITERARY STRUCTURES OF BIBLICAL BOOKS

One approach that many editions took to representing literary structure was to insert section headings into the biblical text. (Many Bibles published today in chapter-and-verse format do this as well, as an aid to readers.) These headings were highlighted and distinguished from the text in various ways: they were capitalized, italicized, centered, or set off by a line of blank space.

Often, however, such headings did not provide an appreciation for a book's overarching structure, because they were used to indicate only lower-level (microstructural) divisions: episodes in historical narratives, individual poetic oracles, teaching or healing pericopae in the gospels, separate points within epistolary discussions, and so forth. In *The New Testament in the Language of Today,* for example, William Beck presented the Sermon on the Mount in nineteen separate sections, corresponding to its most specific topical concerns, e.g. "Don't Blow Your Horn" (almsgiving, Matthew 6:1-4), "How to Pray" (6:5-15) and "Fasting" (6:16-18). Detailed indications of microstructure like this can be helpful, but they fail to identify the Sermon on the Mount as a unified extended discourse that represents one of the highest-level literary sections within Matthew.

But in other cases, publishers did use headings to indicate such macrostructural literary divisions within biblical books. The Sermon on the Mount comprised just a single one of the large sections into which Alexander Campbell divided Matthew in *The Sacred Writings*.[28] And Theophile J. Meek similarly used headings as macrostructural indicators in his translation of the Pentateuch for the Smith-Goodspeed Bible. He identified Leviticus 1-7 as a single section, for example, entitling it "Laws Relating to Sacrifice."[29]

In both of these editions, however, the text within these larger sections was simply divided into paragraphs. Readers were therefore not helped to recognize whether any intermediate-sized literary-structural units might lie in between macrostructural sections and paragraphs (for example, the separate groups of laws in Leviticus 1-7 relating to different types of sacrifices: burnt, grain, fellowship, sin and guilt offerings). But other editions that provided section headings indicative of literary macrostructure did also mark intermediate structural divisions, through a variety of means.

In *The Message*, for example, when larger literary sections were marked by headings, smaller units within those sections were set off by a Jerusalem cross. Thus Paul's entire discussion of food offered to idols

---

28.   Campbell, pp. 61-66. Campbell did not insert headings into every book, but only included them when he felt they were appropriate to genre: "In the four Narratives of the Life of the Lord Jesus, we have followed the sectional divisions of the translator [George Campbell, 1778], which in no place interferes with the sense of any passage. In histories it is easy to make such divisions as do not impair or obscure the narrative. Besides, all histories, ancient and modern, are so arranged. But in the Epistles such divisions are not to be expected; nor are they so compatible with epistolary as historic compositions." "General Preface," http://www.mun.ca/rels/restmov/oracles1st/preface.html.

29.   *The Complete Bible: An American Translation*, pp. 90ff. (OT). However, the other scholars who cooperated on this translation typically used headings to mark microstructural divisions.

in 1 Corinthians 8-10 was introduced by the heading "Freedom With Responsibility," while the beginnings of the second and third parts of this discussion were marked by crosses.

Richard Moulton used an even more elaborate and varied system in his *Modern Reader's Bible*. In the historical narratives he used centered headings to identify large sections such as "The Kingdom of Judah to Its Captivity" (that is, the reigns of Hezekiah through Zedekiah, 2 Kings 18:1-25:30). He marked the reigns of individual kings in this section by putting their names in bold type in marginal cutouts. And he indicated the individual episodes of these reigns through paragraphing. But Moulton used different conventions in other parts of the Bible. He divided Ezekiel, for example, into seven "books"; he marked each of the oracles in these "books" with Roman numerals and summary headings; and he divided the parts of these oracles from one another with large centered asterisks.

Moulton explained that his goal had been to "investigate . . . the exact literary form and detailed structure of the books of Scripture; and then to use all the devices of modern printing for the purpose of indicating such structure to the eye of the reader."[30] But in some parts of his volume, there can be a feeling of diminishing returns, as Moulton uses perhaps not all, but a great many, of the "devices of modern printing" at once. As valuable as it is to help readers appreciate literary structure in the biblical books, any apparatus inserted into the text of Scripture should not become so complicated or distracting that the flow of reading is interrupted and the overall goal of promoting reading with greater understanding and enjoyment is thwarted.

Some other editions seem to have struck a more successful balance between providing literary-structural guidance and maintaining readability by using inserted headings only to indicate macrostructure, and then marking off smaller literary units more subtly and implicitly. In *The New English Bible*, a centered, italicized heading identified "The Sermon

---

30. Moulton, p. vii.

on the Mount" as one of the highest-level sections in Matthew. The Sermon itself was then divided into five parts of intermediate size. (One of them, for instance, comprised the related discussions of the practice of piety that Beck had presented as three separate smaller sections on almsgiving, prayer and fasting.) The editors identified these intermediate parts only by inserting one blank line beforehand and by setting the opening words in small caps. Paragraphing marked off the smaller units within these parts.

The Twentieth Century New Testament used a very similar convention, but in such a way that it could indicate even more levels of literary structure. A heading identified one macrostructural division of 1 Corinthians as "Answers to Questions about Marriage and Heathen Feasts" (7:1-11:1). Paul discusses each of these topics in phases, and each of these phases were set off in this edition by one line of white space. They were then subdivided into paragraphs. But the two larger topical discussions themselves were separated from each other by two lines of white space. Four levels of literary structure were thus indicated (the large macrostructural division; its two constituent discussions; the phases of these discussions; and the paragraphs within each phase). But only one heading was used, for the highest level; indentation and variable spacing showed how the smaller literary units were nested within the larger ones.

We may note in passing that a minority view of the macrostructure of 1 Corinthians is actually represented at this point in *The Twentieth Century New Testament.* A majority of interpreters would not combine the two topics of "marriage" and "heathen feasts" into a single section, but would instead use Paul's recurring introductory formula "now about" (*peri de*) to identify three sections relating to married couples (7:1-24), the unmarried (7:25-40) and food sacrificed to idols (8:1-11:1). However, the issue of how literary structure is to be *identified* will be taken up in the Appendix. Our concern here is with how literary structure is to be *indicated* in the books of the Bible. And in that light, the convention employed in *The Twentieth Century New Testament* is exemplary for our consideration. It shows how multiple levels of structure, such as its editors saw here, may be indicated effectively and unobtrusively.

Indeed, this example raises the interesting question of whether any edition has subdivided the books of the Bible without using any printed headings at all. At least one has: Richmond Lattimore's translation of the New Testament. In that volume, the start of a new section is indicated only by one blank line and the symbol ⁋ before the opening words. However, Lattimore used this convention only to divide books according to the traditional chapter breaks. Readers were thus encouraged to try to understand the Bible "naturally" (that is, without being directed by intrusive numbers) as if chapter divisions corresponded reliably with literary structure. This cannot have been practical in many places. Nevertheless, the complete omission of inserted headings in Lattimore's translation presents an attractive approach to indicating more appropriate divisions within the biblical text.

BOOK BOUNDARIES

Removing chapter and verse numbers from the text of scripture and providing more reliable indications of literary structure are already significant steps towards overcoming the way traditional elements can obscure form and meaning in the Scriptures. But as we saw in Chapter Two, there are some additional factors on the book level that can also interfere with readers' understanding.

One of these is the way some of the longer works have been divided into parts that are now treated as complete in themselves. While there are many different ways in which chapter and verse numbers may be muted or literary structure indicated, there seems to be a simple and unique solution to the problem of divided books: putting them back together. And some of the editions we have been discussing did take steps in that direction.

While Ernest Sutherland Bates, for example, did not recombine any works in *The Bible Designed to be Read as Living Literature*, he did caution in his book introductions that some longer works within the Bible had been divided. He wrote that Genesis, for example, is not "properly a separate book at all," but part of a larger "compilation."[31] He noted similarly in his introduction to 2 Kings that the "division between the First and Second Books of the Kings is purely artificial, as there is no break in the narrative or alteration of point of view."[32] And he described the book of Acts as "a continuation of the Gospel according to Luke," written by "the same author."[33]

Other editions did go so far as to present the rejoined parts of divided works as single books once again. In *The Original New Testament*, Hugh Schonfield put Luke's two volumes back together under the title "A History of Christian Beginnings." "Part I: How the Good New Came to Israel" corresponded with the gospel of Luke, and "Part II: How the Good New Came to the Gentiles" consisted of the book of Acts.[34] And in *The Modern Reader's Bible*, Richard Moulton presented a single book called "The Chronicles" that included 1 Chronicles, 2 Chronicles, Ezra and Nehemiah.[35]

However, while these three editions did promote the reintegration of some works, they actually disintegrated other ones. Schonfield created four separate letters out of Paul's Corinthian correspondence, putting selections from 1 and 2 Corinthians into the first, the rest of 1 Corinthians in the second, the end of 2 Corinthians in the third, and the rest of 2 Corinthians in the fourth. Bates divided Isaiah into two books. He called the second one "The Rhapsodies of the Unknown Prophet" and put six other books between it and what was left of Isaiah. Moulton similarly created a separate book from the end of Isaiah that he called "Zion Redeemed." He also split off the closing oracles of Zechariah and put them with Malachi in a book of "Anonymous Prophecies."

---

31. Bates, p. 2. Bates actually considered the "compilation" of which Genesis formed a part to be the "Hexateuch," meaning the Pentateuch plus Joshua.

32. Ibid., p. 327.

33. Ibid., p. 1043.

34. Schonfield, pp. 125-169.

35. Moulton, pp. 387-468.

The new divisions that Moulton, Bates and Schonfield introduced into biblical works did not, like the more traditional divisions, reflect limitations of scroll length; these had long been transcended. Rather, they reflected the presuppositions of source criticism: that one could look behind the finished form of some biblical writings and trace their composition history, which had presumably involved the combination of originally separate works into a somewhat ungainly final product whose seams were still showing. Those who created these new divisions, however, did not observe or respect the literary-structural patterns that may actually be seen to hold together, quite elegantly, the books into which they introduced these divisions. (These are discussed in the introductions to each of these works in *The Books of The Bible*.) An examination of this patterning suggests that 1 and 2 Corinthians are not actually recombinations of up to four separate letters. It also suggests that even if later prophets have added their oracles to those of Isaiah and Zechariah (this is a matter of ongoing debate even among scholars who hold to the inspiration of the Scriptures), new, integrated volumes have successfully been created from the collected prophecies.

Nor did some of the ways in which Moulton recombined historical books other than Chronicles-Ezra-Nehemiah respect the patterns that, I would argue, hold them together in larger units than the traditional book divisions, but in smaller units than he ultimately created. Moulton's divisions were based largely on historical content, despite the literary goals of his edition. He divided the long narrative that runs from Genesis through Kings into four main parts, corresponding to four periods in Israelite history:

Genesis ("the formation of the chosen nation");

Exodus-Leviticus-Numbers ("the migration of the chosen nation to the land of promise");

Joshua-Judges-Ruth-1 Samuel[36] ("the chosen nation in its efforts towards a secular government"); and

---

36.   Moulton actually included the opening of 2 Samuel, through the end of David's lament for Saul and Jonathan, in this section. See Moulton, pp. 2-3.

2 Samuel-1 Kings-2 Kings ("the chosen nation under a kingship side by side with a theocracy").

Deuteronomy, as a work in a clearly distinct genre, was allowed to punctuate this otherwise continuous national saga.

But historical and literary considerations, I would argue, suggest that Moulton could appropriately have put the boundary between "The Judges" and "The Kings" at the start of Samuel instead. Even under Saul, the "chosen nation" was "under a kingship side by side with a theocracy," and the "antagonism of kings and prophets" that Moulton says "makes the main history of Israel"[37] was certainly evident in the interactions between Samuel and Saul. Beyond this, 1 Samuel shares with the rest of Samuel-Kings a literary-structural formula based on regnal information, while Joshua and Judges employ different formulae (e.g., in the case of the latter, "Again the Israelites did evil in the eyes of the LORD"). In other words, historical and literary considerations indeed complement one another in this long narrative section of the Old Testament, and so, I would argue, segmenting it essentially by history does not do full justice to the literature.

Once again, however, we find ourselves discussing how literary structure in the Bible may be *identified,* a concern that is taken up in the Appendix. Let us therefore conclude this discussion of how book boundaries may rather be *indicated* by noting that the simple expedient of recombination has already been used by some publications in the cases of Luke-Acts and Chronicles-Ezra-Nehemiah, and that this suggests an appropriate model for Samuel-Kings as well.

BOOK SEQUENCE

Another book-level factor that can create difficulties for readers of the Bible is the traditional sequence. This, as we have seen, can create misleading expectations about literary genre, and discourage reading with an appreciation for a book's historical circumstances of composition.

---

37.   Moulton, p. ix.

The editors of some of the Bibles, testaments and portions we have been considering in this chapter also sought to help readers overcome these effects. Appropriately, they tended to use a combination of literary and historical criteria to reorder the biblical books.

Hugh Schonfield explained in his introduction to *The Original New Testament* that

> [t]he order in which the books appear in the ecclesiastical versions
> is not an order of publication, but largely of type and to an extent of
> authority: Gospels, Acts, Epistles, Revelation. But in arranging the
> elements for general and intelligent reading, certain changes in order
> are obviously desirable, first to keep together those documents which
> are in some way associated, and second to give some consideration to
> chronological sequence. Commonsense requires that the Gospel of
> John should not be sandwiched between the two parts of Luke's work,
> the Gospel and Acts. Nor should the Gospel of John be separated
> from the Letters of John. Equally a rational editing of Paul's letters
> requires that they be placed as far as possible in chronological order.[38]

In order to promote "intelligent reading," Schonfield therefore changed both the grouping and the order of the books. The gospels in their likely chronological order (Mark, Matthew, Luke, John) provided the pillars for the overall structure he gave the New Testament. But he grouped related books with each gospel, so that after Mark and Matthew came Luke-Acts together with Paul's letters, in what he considered their chronological order. The general epistles followed, once again in their presumed chronological order, and finally the gospel and epistles of John, with Revelation.

The editors of *The Twentieth Century New Testament* wrestled similarly with how they might balance considerations of genre and chronology as they sought to help readers overcome the difficulties that the traditional book sequence could create. They explained in their introduction:

---

38.   Schonfield, pp. xxxi-xxxii

In early times very great variety prevailed in the arrangement of the books of the New Testament. The order depended partly on their length, partly on the relative importance of the cities to which they were addressed, still more on the different degrees of authority attributed to the writers. . . . It might, at first sight, appear best, in a translation intended principally for general readers, to keep to the common order, but this would help to perpetuate an arrangement which greatly hinders the comprehension of the Pauline Letters, placing, as it does, the earlier ones after those written in later years. On the other hand, to put the whole of the books in the order of their composition (in which the "Epistle of James" would probably stand at the beginning and the "Gospel according to John" at the end, and in which Historical Books and Letters would be curiously mixed) would be an arrangement . . . more puzzling than helpful.

It has been thought best, therefore, to retain the usual grouping [gospels, Acts, Pauline epistles, general epistles, Revelation], but arrange the books contained in each group in chronological order."[39]

This edition therefore presented the books of the New Testament in this sequence:

The Four Gospels and the Acts:
  Mark, Matthew, Luke, John, Acts
St. Paul's Letters to the Churches:
  Group I: 1 Thessalonians, 2 Thessalonians
  Group II: Romans, 1 Corinthians, 2 Corinthians, Galatians
  Group III: Ephesians, Philippians, Colossians
Pastoral, Personal and General Letters
  Group I, Pastoral Letters: 1 Timothy, 2 Timothy, Titus[40]

---

39. *The Twentieth Century New Testament*, pp. v-vi.

40. F.F. Bruce, it may be noted, put the Pauline epistles in a similar order in *The Letters of Paul: An Expanded Paraphrase* (Grand Rapids: Eerdmans, 1965):

I. Earlier Epistles: Galatians, 1 Thessalonians, 2 Thessalonians

II. The Middle Years: 1 Corinthians, 2 Corinthians, Philippians

III. The Gospel According to Paul: Romans

IV. Paul in Rome: Colossians, Philemon, Ephesians

Group II, Personal Letters: Philemon, 2 John, 3 John
Group III, General Letters: Hebrews, James, 1 John, 1 Peter,
2 Peter, Jude
Revelation

So editors and translators have reorganized the books of the New Testament in different ways in an attempt to promote greater understanding. This has also been done for the Scriptures as a whole. In *The Modern Reader's Bible*, Richard Moulton used literary genre as his primary organizing principle as he regrouped, and thus reordered, all of the biblical books.

Moulton sorted the Old Testament books into four groups: History, Prophets, Poetry and Wisdom. Within the History section, chronology was a secondary organizing principle. While Moulton made some recombinations of the historical books from Genesis through Kings (as we have just seen above), he nevertheless left this series of books in its traditional order, since it was already chronological. He placed Esther (and the apocryphal book of Tobit) after Kings as "stories of the exile." And he concluded this section with Chronicles-Ezra-Nehemiah, which reached into the post-exilic period. In the Prophets section, however, Moulton did not use history as a secondary organizing principle. Instead, he simply left the books books in their traditional, non-chronological order. He grouped Psalms, Lamentations and Song of Songs together in his Poetry section, allowing readers to recognize each book, by comparison with the others, as a collection of lyric poetry. He similarly created a section of Wisdom writings containing Proverbs, Ecclesiastes and Job (plus two apocryphal works, Ecclesiasticus and Wisdom of Solomon).

Moulton arranged the books of the New Testament so that it started, like the Old, with an extended historical section. He placed Luke-Acts first and inserted Paul's first six epistles right into the text of this narrative, at the times when he believed they were written. Paul's

---

V. Pastoral Epistles: Titus, 1 Timothy, 2 Timothy.

remaining epistles, similarly in chronological order, were attached to the end of the narrative. The general epistles then followed, so that epistles actually made up more than half of this "History" section. A second New Testament group, "Other Books," included Matthew, Mark, John and Revelation. (Moulton first published *The Modern Reader's Bible* in twenty-one separate volumes, organized into five series: History, Wisdom, Poetry, Prophecy and New Testament. His grouping of the books in the New Testament Series appears, in retrospect, more successful than the arrangement he finally adopted for his one-volume edition. He issued a two-volume collection of Luke-Acts and Paul's letters; a single volume that contained the "Gospel, Epistles and Revelation of St. John"; and placed Matthew, Mark and the general epistles in a final volume. He was thus following the broad principle of "keep[ing] together those documents which are in some way associated" that Schonfield would later advocate in *The Original New Testament*.)

Moulton's order, when compared with the traditional one, does highlight literary genre in significant ways, not least because it treats generic collections as moveable groups (the prophets as a whole are transferred from the end of the Old Testament to the middle, and the works that customarily come between the prophetic and historical books are sorted into poetry and wisdom clusters). Nevertheless, it seems fair to observe that Moulton was not consistent in his use of literary genre as an organizing principle in *The Modern Reader's Bible*. Instead, he used it interchangeably with chronology, but did not give clear priority to either. If the prophets were to be grouped together based on genre, for example, but then presented in the traditional order, why were Paul's epistles also not left as a group, in the traditional sequence, rather than sorted by chronology and combined with a historical narrative? On the other hand, if Paul's epistles were to be treated that way, why weren't the prophetic books put in their chronological sequence and inserted at appropriate places in the extended Old Testament historical narrative? Perhaps this inconsistency was one reason why Ernest Sutherland Bates wrote, in his introduction to *The Bible Designed to be Read as Living Literature*, that while he considered

Moulton's volume the "most successful" attempt that had yet been made to "clothe the Bible in a dress through which its beauty might shine best," "neither [Moulton] nor any of his successors quite accomplished their aim."[41]

Bates, however, apparently instructed both positively and negatively by the example of Moulton and others, was able to use first genre, and then chronology, more consistently to order the biblical books in his own edition. He explained in his introduction that his goal was to gather the books in each testament into literary groups, and then within those groups "to print all the works in the order of their composition."[42] His Old Testament sections are reminiscent of Moulton's: "Historical Books," "Prophetical Books," and then "Poetry, Drama, Fiction, and Philosophy." He was able to leave the books in his first group (Genesis through Nehemiah) in their traditional sequence, which was already chronological, although he moved Ruth to his third section, and chose to omit Chronicles from his abridged edition of the Scriptures. He then presented the prophets in what he understood to be their historical order: Amos, Hosea, Micah, Isaiah, Zephaniah, Nahum, Habakkuk, Jeremiah, Ezekiel, Obadiah, Haggai, Zechariah, Joel and Malachi. (He included Lamentations after Jeremiah because of its subject matter, but moved Jonah to his third section, and, in the belief that the second part of Isaiah was written by a later prophet, actually located that part of the book after Ezekiel.) In the final group he classified Psalms and Proverbs as poetry (he considered Proverbs specifically an "anthology of gnomic poetry"); Job, Ecclesiastes and Song of Songs as drama; Ruth, Jonah, Daniel, and Esther (along with Judith, Susanna and Tobit) as "tales"; and Ecclesiasticus and Wisdom of Solomon as "philosophy." Within each of these subgroups, the books were placed in the presumed "order of their composition."

---

41.   Bates, pp. ix-x. The quotation about "clothing" the Bible is from Sir Arthur Quiller-Couch's lecture "On Reading the Bible (II)," http://www.bartleby.com/191/9.html.

42.   Bates, p. xii.

Although Bates did not define similar sections within the New Testament, he nevertheless sorted its books clearly into generic groups as well: gospels, in the order Mark, Matthew, Luke, John; Acts; selected Pauline and general epistles (in chronological order in each subgroup); and lastly the book of Revelation. Whether or not this particular arrangement was actually the one through which the Bible's beauty could shine "best," it was certainly a clear, consistent and informative way of ordering the biblical books.

Indeed, the most appropriate way to address this traditional factor may not be to try to create the best possible new sequence to displace the existing one, but rather to return to the fluidity of book order that prevailed for the first three quarters of the full Bible's history. If the biblical books may be arranged in a variety of ways, their presentation can suit different goals that translators, editors and publishers wish to pursue.

BOOK TITLES

Finally, the traditional titles constitute a third book-level factor that can make it more difficult for readers to understand the Bible. Editors and publishers have expanded upon or altered some of these. In certain cases, however, the changes they made simply reinforced the expectations the customary titles already encouraged. In *The Sacred Writings*, for example, Alexander Campbell used lengthened titles that included an attribution of authorship and thus assigned the book of Matthew to "Matthew Levi, the apostle," Hebrews to "Paul the Apostle," and Revelation to "the Apostle John." We noted in Chapter Two, however, that there are good reasons to believe that each of these books may not have been written by the author suggested.

But in other cases, editors and publishers made title changes that encouraged alternatives to traditional interpretations of genre, audience and authorship. For example, we saw in Chapter Two how identifying James simply as an epistle can lead readers to have the wrong expectations about its genre. Richard Moulton therefore entitled it "The

Wisdom Epistle of St. James," highlighting its affinities with other works in the wisdom tradition. And since the term "gospel" does not so much refer to a specific literary genre as to the content of the books known by this title, the *Twentieth Century New Testament* and *The New Testament in the Language of Today* substituted the phrase "good news" for the term "gospel." Campbell, for his part, used the word "testimony," similarly placing the emphasis on the fact of witness and proclamation, rather than suggesting literary genre.[43] As we also observed in Chapter Two, there are good reasons to believe that the letter we know as Ephesians may not actually have been sent to believers in Ephesus. It may instead have been either the letter to Laodicea mentioned at the end of Colossians, or else a circular letter sent to a group of churches in Asia Minor. To reflect this second possibility, *The Original New Testament* entitled Ephesians "To the Communities in Asia (The Ephesian Copy)."[44] J.B. Phillips, for his part, called it "The Letter to the Christians at Ephesus (and In Other Places)." To offer a final example, Richard Moulton, aware that "Malachi" means "my messenger" and that the opening of the book of Malachi may therefore be a "subject title" (i.e. "An oracle: the word of the LORD to Israel by the hand of my messenger"), described the book as one of several "Anonymous Prophecies."[45]

However, in cases like these the new title simply substituted a different interpretation for the traditional one, rather than suggesting that the traditional interpretation should be held as one possibility among other reasonable ones. This is one hazard of renaming books. Another is that once the book title genie is let out of the bottle, there appears to be no limit on what books might be called. *The Twentieth Century New Testament* entitled the second volume of Luke's history "The Doings of

---

43.　Campbell, pp. 57, 106, 138, 191.

44.　Schonfield, p. 383.

45.　Moulton noted, significantly, that the Septuagint translated the title of this book "simply as 'angel'" (*angelos*, Greek for "messenger"). He suggested that it was only "in process of time" that "'Malachi' was read as a personal name" (p. 1414).

the Apostles."[46] *The Original New Testament* named it "The Acts of the Envoys."[47] And J. B. Phillips, building on a suggestion from C. S. Lewis, famously called it *The Young Church in Action.*[48]

Acts was not the only book to inspire such creativity. J. B. Phillips retitled Hebrews "The Letter to Jewish Christians," while Hugh Schonfield called it the "Homily on the High Priesthood of Christ." He also retitled John "The Discourses of the Logos." Moulton, as we saw earlier, entitled the second part of Isaiah "The Rhapsody of Zion Redeemed," while Bates called it "The Rhapsodies of the Unknown Prophet." Bates used the first lines of the other prophetic books as their titles, e.g. "The word of the Lord that came unto Hosea," "The vision of Nahum the Elkohite," "The burden of Habakkuk." In this way he applied the earliest tradition for naming the books of the Pentateuch to the prophetic works. But he did not return to the practice of calling the books of the Pentateuch after their opening words ("In the Beginning," etc.); he simply retained their customary titles (Genesis, Exodus, etc.).

The greatest danger of too much license to change book titles is that readers and students of the Bible will lose a common frame of reference. How is a reader of "The Testimony of John the Apostle" to know that "The Discourses of the Logos" is the same book? Or how would groups studying "The Letter to Jewish Christians" or "The Homily on the High Priesthood of Christ" know that a commentary on the book of Hebrews would be a helpful resource for them? The challenge for those who would rename the biblical books therefore seems to be this: providing enough continuity with the tradition to allow readers who already have some familiarity with the Bible to recognize books, but at the same

---

46.   *The Twentieth Century New Testament*, p. 198.

47.   Schonfield, p. 201.

48.   J.B. Phillips, trans., *The Young Church in Action: A New Translation of the Acts* (London: Geoffrey Bles, 1955). Phillips acknowledges Lewis for suggesting the title *Letters to Young Churches* for his translation of the New Testament epistles (*The New Testament in Modern English*, p. xi).

time keeping a range of traditional and nontraditional interpretive possibilities open for all readers.

CONCLUSION: WHY HAS THE TRADITIONAL PRESENTATION CONTINUED TO PREDOMINATE?

When we consider how many different editions of the Bible, going back at least 300 years, have taken measures to help readers overcome the influence of traditional factors, we may well wonder why the standard presentation of the Scriptures continues to be in two columns, with chapter and verse numbers inserted into the text, with the larger books divided into separate parts and all of the books set in a confusing order, bearing potentially misleading names. In short, why hasn't the approach to formatting the Bible represented in the editions we have considered in this chapter caught on?

One possibility is that many of these editions were private translations, done by an individual or a small group, rather than by authorized committees of scholars. The editions by Beck, Phillips, Lattimore, Moffatt, Schonfield, Torrey and Weymouth all represented individual translations. For *The Sacred Writings*, as we have seen, Alexander Campbell combined individual translations of three different portions of the New Testament. The so-called Smith-Goodspeed Bible (*An American Translation*) was the work of one translator for the New Testament and four for the Old. *The Twentieth Century New Testament*, according to its own introduction, was "undertaken as a labor of love, by a company of about twenty persons . . . without authority from Church or State."[49] And *The Message* by Eugene Peterson was a paraphrase.

However, some of the editions we have been considering did use the text of major committee translations that had a degree of ecclesiastical authority. Moulton, for example, used the English Revised Version of 1885 (although he made his own choices between "the readings of the

---

49.   *The Twentieth Century New Testament*, p. vii.

text and margin"[50]). That version, an official revision of the King James Bible, was the fruit of a decade's work by over a hundred British and American scholars. Bates, for his part, used the King James itself. And *The New English Bible* was "planned and directed by representatives" of nine British denominations and two Bible societies and was the work of nearly fifty scholars, who served on four panels under the direction of a Joint Committee. So the approach illustrated by the editions in this chapter has not necessarily failed to become more popular simply because of the individuality of some of the translations.

Another possible explanation is that the Bible was presented in non-traditional formats by people who did not believe in the inspiration and authority of the Scriptures, and that their editions were therefore not considered trustworthy by those who looked to the Bible as the word of God. This description does apply to some of the editors whose work we have considered in this chapter.

We have noted, for example, that *The Bible Designed to be Read as Living Literature* was an abridgment of the Scriptures. Its editor, Ernest Sutherland Bates, explained that his abridgment was actually based on the premise that it was "no longer possible to regard the Bible as the literal word of God"[51] and that "for literary appreciation, one wants not all the Bible but the best of it."[52] Based on his own judgment of what was "best," Bates eliminated some entire books, and large portions of many others. This was not, in other words, a reverent abbreviation, but an attempt to substitute literary artistry for divine inspiration as the grounds for the Bible's enduring claim on human hearts and minds.

To cite another example, readers who were already familiar with the name of Hugh Schonfield may have been uncomfortable with the frequent appeals made here to the volume he edited and translated, *The Original New Testament.* This is because Schonfield was also the

---

50. Moulton, p. xi.
51. Bates, p. vi.
52. Ibid., p. xi.

author of *The Passover Plot*,[53] which alleged that Jesus tried to fake his own death and resurrection in order to fulfill prophecies and establish himself as the Messiah. According to Schonfield, this "plot" failed only when Jesus was unexpectedly speared on the cross by a Roman soldier, suffering a fatal wound from which he could not recover!

However, Bates and Schonfield represent only a small minority among the editors whose work we have been considering. By and large this group honored and respected the Scriptures. In the introduction to *An American Translation,* for example, Edgar Goodspeed wrote that

> the great messages of the Old and New Testaments were never more necessary than in our present confused and hurried life. We have, therefore, sought to produce a new translation of them . . . in the hope that, through its usage, the literary appreciation, the historical understanding, and the religious influence of the Bible may be furthered in our generation.[54]

J.B. Phillips wrote in his translator's preface to *The Young Church in Action* (Acts) that he hoped "those intellectuals who assume that Christianity was founded on a myth in the first place and is in any case a spent force today" would "especially . . . read and study this book," since it would take "more than a little explaining away" on their part.[55] And Alexander Campbell expressed his confidence in the inspiration of the Scriptures when he wrote, at the end of his preface to *The Sacred Writings,* "May all, who honestly examine this version, abundantly partake of the blessings of that Spirit which guided the writers of this volume, and which in every page breathes, 'Glory to God in the highest heaven, peace on earth, and good will among men.' "[56]

---

53. Hugh J. Schonfield, *The Passover Plot* (New York: Random House, 1965).

54. Edgar J. Goodspeed, Preface to *The Complete Bible: An American Translation,* p. v.

55. Phillips, *The Young Church,* pp. viii–ix.

56. Campbell, p. xi.

So we should not associate a presentation of the Bible that seeks to help readers overcome the effects of traditional elements with a skeptical, disrespectful attitude towards the Scriptures themselves. Indeed, it is rather an expression of deep respect for the Bible to seek to present it in a format in which it may speak its own message more clearly.

Moreover, we may learn even from the efforts of those editors who did not actually acknowledge the authority or embrace the teachings of the Bible. It is to be hoped, for example, that those who do respect the Bible as the inspired word of God will give the entire Scriptures as appealing a presentation as Bates did for the portions he selected. And while Schonfield's reconstruction of the events of Christ's life is wildly fanciful, his observations about book order in the New Testament, already noted above, are still perfectly sensible:

> Commonsense requires that the Gospel of John should not be sandwiched between the two parts of Luke's work, the Gospel and Acts. Nor should the Gospel of John be separated from the Letters of John. Equally a rational editing of Paul's letters requires that they be placed as far as possible in chronological order.[57]

There may be another reason why the approach illustrated in this chapter has not yet become the standard presentation of the Scriptures. While each of the traditional elements that affects our understanding and enjoyment of the Bible was addressed by one or more of the editions we have considered, few of these editions undertook to address most or all of these elements at once. Even those who did the most still did not do as much as is represented in the group as a whole. In Lattimore's translation of the New Testament, for example, chapter and verse numbers were removed from the page, with only a range provided at the top, and divisions within books were indicated only by white space, yielding an eminently readable text. But the books were still divided according to chapters, and they were presented in the

---

57.   Schonfield, p. xxxi-xxxii.

traditional order, with Luke and Acts separated by John (even though Lattimore acknowledged that Acts "can be regarded as a continuation of *The Gospel According to Luke*"[58]), with Paul's epistles in order of length, and with James described and formatted as a "letter." In *The Bible Designed to be Read as Living Literature,* Bates removed chapter and verse numbers from the page entirely, and he changed the order of the books significantly. But he still did not recombine the separated parts of longer works, and his extensive deletions from individual books showed little respect for their literary structures and the authorial signals that indicated them.

It is possible, therefore, that we have simply been awaiting an edition of the Scriptures in a major committee translation, produced by those who honor and respect the Bible as the inspired word of God, that addresses all of the traditional elements at once that can affect our understanding and enjoyment of the Scriptures. If that is the case, then it may be hoped that *The Books of The Bible* will not just help many readers have a more meaningful encounter with God's word, but that it will also help the church as a whole to reconsider whether the now-customary format of the Scriptures is indeed the most appropriate way to present the word of God to the people of God.

All of this said, there is still one further possibility we must consider. It may simply be that we retain the Bible in its familiar form because that form is best suited to our habits of reading—or, I should say, our habit of not reading. For however we approach the Bible, it is not usually as a collection of literary works that must each be read through in order to be understood and enjoyed.

Chapters and verses were never intended to guide devotional reading. They were rather introduced, as we saw in Chapter One, so that scholarly resources such as commentaries and concordances could be developed. But now our habits of devotional reading are largely shaped by chapters and verses. We typically approach the Bible as if it were a compendium

---

58. Lattimore, *Acts and Letters,* p. vii.

of well-phrased uplifting sentiments, like *Bartlett's Familiar Quotations*.[59] Or we consider it a volume of short inspiring daily readings, like *Chicken Soup for the Soul*.[60] We may be so captive to these approaches, in fact, that we would regard with suspicion or even hostility any presentation of the Scriptures that we could not easily use in these ways. This may be the true explanation for why more literary formats of the Bible have not yet displaced the chapter-and-verse grid. But this simply means that our habits of reading must change.

The books of the Bible must be recognized, presented and approached for what they are: books. This does not mean that we cannot still read the Bible in appropriate portions, in keeping with the demands of our daily schedules. It does not mean that we cannot cite eloquent phrases that summarize vital parts of the Bible's message, even treasuring those words in our hearts and committing them to memory. But we must appreciate the smaller portions of the biblical books as parts of larger literary wholes, which we first engage in their entirety. When we do, we will find that we can still read portions and cite phrases, but do so far more appropriately and meaningfully.

It has been with the goal of presenting the Bible as the collection of literary works it truly is that the International Bible Society has developed and is now releasing *The Books of The Bible*. (The story of this edition will be told in the final chapter of this book.) Our hope is that this new presentation will enable readers to engage the word of God with greater understanding and enjoyment, and that it will allow them to find their own place in the story that begins in the Bible and continues to this day. And if, for all of this to happen, there needs to be a revolution in our reading habits, then . . . let that revolution begin.

---

59. *Bartlett's Familiar Quotations: A Collection of Passages, Phrases, and Proverbs Traced to Their Sources in Ancient and Modern Literature*, 17th ed. (New York: Little, Brown and Company, 2002).

60. Jack Canfield and Mark Victor Hansen, *Chicken Soup for the Soul: 101 Stories to Open the Heart and Rekindle the Spirit* (Deerfield Beach, Florida: Health Communications, Inc., 1994).

4

The Books of The Bible

WHY AND HOW THIS EDITION WAS CREATED

Literally millions of Bibles are distributed in North America each year, but relatively few of them are ever read. This was the sobering conclusion reached by publishers, demographers and literacy advocates who conducted research on Bible reading late in the 1990s and in the early years of the new century.

Some of the reasons why people weren't reading the Bible reflected larger social trends. In a post-Christian society, they were much less likely to hear the Bible being read aloud, quoted or used in illustrations. So it was an unfamiliar book. Moreover, the prevailing postmodern world view, which embraced pluralism and relativism and was skeptical of absolute truth claims, created hesitations about a book that claimed to be the word of God.

However, there was also a much more practical reason why the Bible was going unread. Even when people actually did open its covers, what they found inside was like no other book they had ever seen before. The text was set in narrow double columns and sprinkled liberally with large and small numbers (indicating chapters and verses) and with superscript italicized letters (signaling footnotes). Many new readers found this format confusing and uninviting. As a result, all the work that had to be done just to get them to pick up a Bible was being wasted.

In fact, even those who were already believers, who felt that they should read the Bible, and wanted to, often reported that their experience with Scripture was spiritually dry and unsatisfying. It didn't keep them coming back for more. It was therefore not surprising that in the United States, while over 90% of homes had a Bible, it was only being read with any degree of regularity in 15% of homes.

This research was of particular concern to Glenn Paauw, director of product development for the U.S. division of the International Bible Society (IBS). Glenn began to reflect on what his department could do to encourage more and better Bible reading. IBS was committed to "scripture-based evangelism" in the recognition that the Bible is the inspired word of God and has inherent power to bring people to salvation and to transform their lives. "Success" for an organization with IBS's mission, therefore, could not be measured simply by the numbers of Bibles being printed and distributed, if lives were not being changed because those Bibles were not being read.

Glenn recognized that some of the reasons why people don't read the Bible couldn't be addressed by publishers alone. But he also knew that in his position he could at least work to present the Bible in a more appealing and accessible form. And so he began to ask, "In what format can the Bible be offered to people who are not reading it, to encourage them to begin reading? And what changes in presentation will help current readers engage the Bible with greater understanding and satisfaction?"

The *People of the Book* series, produced at IBS under Glenn's direction, represented an early expression of this vision for a more readable Bible. In separate volumes published from 2000 through 2003, this series used Scripture text printed without chapter or verse numbers to tell the life stories of individual biblical characters (David; Moses; Abraham, Isaac and Jacob; Women of the Old Testament; and Jesus). But the stories were divided into "chapters" of another kind: they corresponded to major episodes and periods in the characters' lives. The volume dedicated to

Jesus in the *People of the Book* series consisted of the entire gospel of Luke. It was thus an individually bound "book of the Bible," organized according to its own internal principles rather than the traditional numbering system.

Another early effort from Glenn's department was the *Encountering Jesus Journal* (2002), which presented selections from the gospels, also with no numbers in the text. The *Encountering Jesus New Testament*, which was developed in parallel with this journal and which followed the same format, was completed and published in 2005.

To pursue his concerns even further, Glenn put together a project team to develop a new format for the whole Bible that could help today's readers appreciate and understand the word of God better on its own terms. For this team he drew on the capable staff of his own department, which included (at various times during the four years that *The Books of The Bible* was in development) editors Lisa Anderson, Paul Berry, John Dunham, Jim Rottenborn and Micah Weiringa. Glenn also engaged some consultants. One of these was John Kohlenberger, president of Blue Heron Bookcraft, a major Bible typesetter, and author or editor of some three dozen Bible reference works. John had been a pioneer in the application of computers to the production of Bible reference works such as concordances. A second consultant was Dr. Gene Rubingh, who had recently retired after thirteen years as vice president for translation at IBS. During those years he coordinated the work of 70 Bible translation teams and conducted workshops around the world in translation techniques, cross-cultural communication and hermeneutics. Before coming to IBS he served as a missionary in Nigeria for a decade and then was an executive with Christian Reformed Church World Missions for nearly two decades.

Glenn approached me to be part of the team as well when he learned of the research, writing and teaching I had done on "the Bible without chapters and verses." I was using this phrase both to warn against the distortions that occur in our interpretations when we treat chapters and verses as intentional units, and also to encourage reading the Bible with an appreciation for the literary genre, literary structure, circumstances of composition and thematic unity of each of its books. These were ideas I had been interested in ever since my undergraduate studies in literature at Harvard. I continued to pursue them in seminary at Gordon-Conwell and in my doctoral program at Boston College, studying and later publishing on the internally-indicated literary structures of several biblical books.[1] In my work as a pastor in the years that followed, as I led Bible studies and adult classes and preached expository sermon series, I had the opportunity to teach through many more biblical books, always with a view toward understanding their inherent designs and presenting them as whole literary works. I consolidated my research and reflections when I taught a course on "The Bible Without Chapters and Verses" at the 1999 Regent College Summer School. Afterwards I wrote up my lectures and made them available on the Internet. When Glenn saw them there (thanks to a referral by a mutual friend), he realized that I shared his vision for a new format of the Bible that would allow its literary beauties and theological truths to shine forth unimpeded by the traditional factors that can obscure them.

Thus the project team, which came to be known as the Bible Design Group, was created. Starting in September 2003, our group held working meetings about every other month for a year and a half, with members pursuing individual assignments in between. Our work together was informed by a variety of resources. These included, for one thing, the Bibles and testaments discussed in Chapter Three. These editions helped us both theoretically, through the discussions in their introductions, and practically, through the formatting approaches they illustrated. We also consulted a wide range of scholarly books, commentaries and articles, which helped inform our eventual decisions about the placement and presentation of individual works within the Bible. But there were also

---

1. "The Structure of the Book of Revelation in Light of Apocalyptic Literary Conventions," *Novum Testamentum* 36 (1994): 373-393; "The Literary Structure of Leviticus," *Journal for the Study of the Old Testament* 70 (1996): 17-32; "Literary Evidences of a Fivefold Structure in the Gospel of Matthew," *New Testament Studies* 43 (1997): 540-551.

some references that were particularly helpful in guiding our thinking about what overall approach we might take. Among these were *The Literary Guide to the Bible*, an anthology of scholarly articles edited by Robert Alter and Frank Kermode; *The New Testament in its Literary Environment* by David Aune; and *How to Read the Bible Book by Book* by Gordon Fee and Douglas Stuart (which appeared shortly before our group first convened).[2] A number of articles also helped shape our strategic thinking, such as "The Greatest Story Never Read" by Gary M. Burge[3] and "Bible Stories for Derrida's Children: Literary Approaches to a Sacred Book" by Leland Ryken.[4]

In his article Ryken described three different approaches that could be taken to formatting the Bible. "One," he wrote, "is to allow the Bible to remain what it is for most readers—a collection of relatively self-contained units, with individual passages experienced mainly as daily devotional readings or the basis of Sunday sermons." We already knew how the fragmentation of the Scriptures kept people from reading with greater enjoyment and understanding, so this was definitely not an option. Ryken observed that a second approach was to "smooth out the rough places, and by selectivity and a uniform prose style make the Bible a continuous narrative." This, we realized, was actually only one example of how a publisher might try to recast the Bible in a contemporary literary form—to bring it to the reader, instead of bringing the reader to it. While we acknowledged the value in approaches that might at least make people more familiar and comfortable with the Bible's content, we recognized that these would not provide a full engagement with the Scriptures. We therefore identified most strongly with the

---

2.   Robert Alter and Frank Kermode, eds, *The Literary Guide to the Bible* (Cambridge, Mass.: Harvard University Press, 1987); David E. Aune, *The New Testament in Its Literary Environment*, Library of Early Christianity 8 (Philadelphia: Westminster Press, 1987); Gordon D. Fee and Douglas Stuart, *How to Read the Bible Book by Book* (Grand Rapids: Zondervan, 2002).

3.   *Christianity Today* August 9, 1999, pp. 45-49.

4.   *Books & Culture*, January/February 1998, pp. 38-41.

third approach Ryken described: "to accept the diversity and ancientness of the [biblical] anthology as it has come to us but to give readers the critical tools of analysis and interpretation that will equip them to cope with individual texts and the book as a whole."[5] Ryken's description of these contrasting approaches helped us articulate the course we wanted to follow and frame the choices we needed to make. We were not going to leave the Bible looking like a "collection of relatively self-contained units," and we were not going to try to turn the Bible into a modern book. Instead, we would seek to present an ancient book in a way that would make it much more accessible to modern readers.

During our year and a half of regular meetings we developed a good idea of what the new format's main features might be. One of our first decisions, agreed upon with little debate, was to set the Bible in a single column and to remove chapter and verse numbers from the text. We recognized that chapters and verses reflected a relatively late stage of tradition, that they typically suggested artificial divisions within biblical books, and that they encouraged disintegrative habits of reading. We did not want to move these numbers to the margins, where readers might still think they should be used for navigation. We would not have been opposed, in fact, to removing them from the page entirely. But we acknowledged the need to allow current readers of the Bible to orient themselves by reference to a system they were already familiar with, and so we decided to place a chapter-and-verse range, in lighter type, at the bottom of each page.

An early decision was also reached to represent the internal divisions of the biblical books without inserting any descriptive headings and, in the end, without using any other marks (such as the asterisks in *The Modern Reader's Bible* or the Jerusalem crosses in *The Message*). We admired the ease of reading fostered by the unobtrusive printing conventions found in such editions as *The Twentieth Century New Testament*, which used line spacing for literary divisions smaller than those indicated by headings,

---

5.   Ibid., p. 40.

and in Lattimore's translation, which used line spacing alone. (The discovery of these volumes somewhat later in our research confirmed a direction we had been inclined to take from the start.) Our approach in preparing *The Books of The Bible* was ultimately to use only white space of varying widths to indicate the biblical books' literary designs, both macrostructural and microstructural. Following a principle of "the higher the division, the wider the space," we used up to four lines in places to indicate the structures of complex books.

The full Bible in Today's New International Version (TNIV) was completed by the Committee on Bible Translation (CBT) and published early in 2005. Because IBS is the copyright holder of the TNIV, our group would have the privilege of using this state-of-the-art translation for the new format we were developing. The TNIV includes italicized sectional headings throughout, "as an aid to the reader." The translators specify in their preface, however, that these headings "are not to be regarded as part of the biblical text."[6] TNIV Bibles may be published without them, and it seemed consistent with our overall purposes not to include these headings, either, in our planned edition.

We found that when the text was set in a single column without chapter and verse numbers or headings, the distinctive ways in which the CBT translators had already represented different literary genres became much more evident. This was visual confirmation for us that chapter and verse divisions, when present, unfortunately do homogenize literary genre. But it also revealed that the Bible, when freed from these traditional elements, displays a variety of beautiful and intricate literary forms. As the TNIV's formatting came to prominence, stories and songs, poems and proverbs, letters and lists filled the pages of the Bible in a way we had not seen before.

The TNIV includes hundreds of notes that clarify terms, provide alternative translations and textual readings, supply modern equiva-

---

6.   Committee on Bible Translation, "A Word to the Reader," *The Holy Bible: Today's New International Version* (Colorado Springs: International Bible Society, 2005), p. v.

lents of ancient weights and measures, and identify the sources of quotations. We recognized that these notes were an essential part of the translation itself and that it was very important for them to be available to readers. At the same time, however, we felt that printing them at the bottom of the page and signaling them within the text by superscript italicized letters would interrupt the continuous reading we wished to encourage. We therefore ultimately decided to present them as end notes after each book, identified by callout phrases, and to signal them subtly within the text with a small raised circle shaded in lighter type.[7]

The creation of endnotes was one specific expression of a general decision we reached early in our discussions: to place all supporting materials outside the actual text of biblical books. We often drew an analogy to the digital video disk (DVD), which allows viewers to access and watch a film by itself, in its entirety, and then separately call up features such as "making of" documentary shorts, interviews with cast and crew, and music videos. We resolved to present the biblical books uninterrupted as whole literary works, but also to provide explanatory "features" outside them in the form of book and section introductions and endnotes. We envisioned even these materials being surrounded by a further layer of information and instruction provided by the believing community. As the Preface to *The Books of The Bible* puts it, "we encourage readers to study the Bible in community, because we believe that if they do, they, their teachers, leaders and peers will provide one

---

7.   There were precedents for this approach to notes in some of the editions discussed in Chapter Three. In *The New Testament in the Language of Today* (St. Louis: Condordia, 1964), William Beck used endnotes after each book to document references to the Old Testament. In *The Modern Reader's Bible* (New York: Macmillan, 1907), Richard Moulton put all of the notes at the back of the volume. He placed no footnote indicators within the text, but instead used chapter and verse references and callout phrases within the notes themselves. For example, in the book of Ruth:

iii. 12. *It is true that I am a near kinsman: howbeit there is a kinsman nearer than I.* The legal custom underlying the story seems to be an extension of what appears in the Mosaic law. . . . The story of Ruth implies that the obligation extended, failing a husband's brother, to whoever was nearest of kin (p. 1555).

another with much more information and many more insights than could ever be included between the covers of a printed Bible."[8]

Beyond these decisions about formatting and presentation, about which we reached durable general conclusions early in our discussions, we recognized several "macro issues" (as we came to call them) relating to book boundaries, sequence and names. It took many more months to settle on approaches to these.

In the case of book boundaries, we concluded in the end that we should recombine Samuel-Kings, Chronicles-Ezra-Nehemiah and Luke-Acts into single books. We might similarly have recombined the five parts of the Torah, but we wanted readers to be able to recognize the way some later biblical writings make allusion to these parts in their literary shapes. We considered these allusions significant for interpretation, and so left Genesis through Deuteronomy as separate books. Nevertheless, we provided a common introduction to Exodus, Leviticus and Numbers to highlight the way they are tied together by a single literary-structural pattern. (Joshua and Judges, which are also closely integrated books, similarly share an introduction). Thus we presented the full contents of the canon in 59 books rather than the traditional 66.

In terms of book names, we concluded after much discussion that the challenge for interpretation presented by the traditional titles of the books of the Bible could best be met by an approach that (1) would provide enough continuity with the tradition to allow readers who already had some familiarity with the Bible to recognize books; (2) would not perpetuate the interpretations of authorship, audience and genre suggested by the traditional titles; and (3) would not simply substitute alternative interpretations for these, but allow readers to consider a range of possibilities. We therefore chose to use the abbreviated titles now in use by many publishers as a kind of shorthand to

---

8.   The Bible Design Group, "Preface," *The Books of The Bible: A Presentation of Today's New International Version* (Colorado Springs: International Bible Society, 2007), p. v.

identify books in a familiar way, without necessarily suggesting that these titles were descriptive of genre, authorship or audience. Thus, for example, "James" and "Acts" rather than "The Epistle of James" and "The Acts of the Apostles"; "Matthew" instead of "The Gospel According to St. Matthew"; "Ephesians," not "The Letter of Paul to the Ephesians."

The question of book order generated some of our most extensive discussions. We felt that the tradition itself provided ample precedents for presenting the biblical books in various orders, depending on the goals of a presentation. In preparing *The Books of The Bible*, our goal was to enable today's readers to engage the Scriptures with greater understanding and enjoyment. In ordering the biblical books we therefore ultimately favored criteria that we felt could help overcome the difficulties that the traditional sequence can now create: misleading expectations about genre, and an underappreciation for circumstances of composition. This meant following an approach that kept together documents that were exemplars of the same genre or products of the same historical milieu. (Often these considerations overlapped, as in the cases of the prophetic and wisdom traditions.) Secondarily, within groups of writings thus defined, we felt that a chronological sequencing would help readers further appreciate the contexts within which biblical works were created.

This meant specifically, in the case of the First Testament (we felt this was an appropriate name for what is commonly known as the Old Testament), presenting the books in three main divisions. As our introduction to the First Testament in *The Books of The Bible* explains:

> The first division, Covenant History, includes not just the books that the Hebrews call the "law" (Genesis–Deuteronomy), but also the books they call the "former prophets" (Joshua–Kings), since all of these books together make up a continuous narrative. It tells the story of God's dealings with humanity from the beginning of the world up to the time when the people of Israel were conquered and sent into exile. The second division presents the books that the Hebrews call the "latter prophets." While these are traditionally divided into two groups according to their size (the long books being considered the "major prophets" and the short ones the "minor prophets"), here

they are presented together in what we believe to be their historical order. The third division contains the "writings." These are grouped according to what kind of literature they are: song lyrics, wisdom, history or apocalypse.[9]

In the New Testament, we grouped together works that seemed to come from the same milieu within the first-century community of Christ's followers. We then worked out what we felt was an appropriate order in which these groups might appear. In the words of the introduction to this testament in *The Books of The Bible*:

> We have reunited the two volumes of Luke-Acts and placed them first because they provide an overview of the New Testament period. This allows readers to see where most of the other books belong. Next come Paul's letters in the order in which we believe they were most likely written. Luke was one of Paul's co-workers in sharing the good news about Jesus, so his volumes are well suited to accompany Paul's letters. The gospel according to Matthew comes next, together with two books, Hebrews and James, also addressed to Jews who believed in Jesus as their Messiah. Then comes the gospel according to Mark (which many scholars believe was actually the first gospel to be written), together with the letters of Peter, since Mark seems to tell the story of Jesus' life from Peter's perspective. Also included in this group is the letter of Jude, which has many similarities with Peter's second letter. Our final group begins with the gospel according to John, which can suitably come last among the gospels because it represents a mature reflection, after many years, on the meaning of Jesus' life. The letters of John follow his gospel. The book of Revelation is appropriately placed last and by itself, since it is unique in literary type and perspective, and it describes how God's saving plan for all of creation will ultimately be realized.[10]

---

9.   *The Books of The Bible*, p. 1.

10.   Ibid., p. 72.

We were delighted to recognize that this manner of presentation was able to "express the ancient concept of the fourfold gospel in a fresh way." In this arrangement,

> The traditional priority of the stories of Jesus is retained, but now each gospel is placed at the beginning of a group of related books. Thus the presentation of four witnesses to the one gospel of Jesus the Messiah is enhanced by a fuller arrangement that will help readers better appreciate why the books of the New Testament were written and what kind of literature they represent.[11]

By the end of our first year of deliberations, we felt we had settled on the basic details of the format we were developing. We knew it was time to share our thinking and ideas with IBS's ministry partners, whose insights would be valuable and helpful.

Over the next year and a half, members of the Committee on Bible Translation and leaders of the Bible publishing divisions at Zondervan Corporation (the commercial distributor of the TNIV) very generously shared their perspectives on the developing edition. With the benefit of their comments and questions, we were able to refine the format even further.

A Preview Edition of the New Testament was prepared late in 2005 and distributed to several hundred reviewers. These included seminary professors, pastors and Christian workers, publishers and editors, and interested people from many other walks of life. A small number of reviewers responded that they were already reading and studying the Bible meaningfully in the customary format and so did not see a need for a change. But the overwhelming majority of those who commented on this preview edition expressed an enthusiasm and even an excitement about the difference that being able to engage the text so much more directly made in their experience with the Bible. One reviewer wrote, "I love it . . . . I found myself understanding the scripture in a new way, with a fresh lens, and I felt spiritually refreshed as a result. I learn much more

---

11.   Ibid.

through stories being told and, with this new format, I felt the truth of the story come alive for me in new ways." Another reported, "I found from personal reading that I drew connections I hadn't drawn before by being forced to read larger chunks." And yet another reviewer wrote:

> I have been a reader of the Bible for all of my life. . . . But after
> reading just a few pages (literally), I was amazed at what I had been
> missing all of these years. For example, even though I "knew" that
> 1 Corinthians was a letter written by Paul, I didn't realize that I
> wasn't reading it as I would a normal letter (until after I read the
> Preview Edition). Suddenly, the contents of the letter made more
> sense—and they fit together.

Such comments were very encouraging, since they suggested that the format changes we had been working on would indeed help foster "more and better Bible reading," as we often described our goal.

Many readers of the Preview Edition offered useful suggestions that we agreed could enhance the presentation even further. The experience of seeing the format in actual print also helped us recognize other improvements that could be made. IBS used the principles developed in the Bible Design Group to create some Scripture resources in advance of the release of a full Bible, including *The Search* (an edition of Ecclesiastes) and *The Journey* (the Gospel of John) in 2005 and *The Book of Psalms* in 2006. As the "wordwrights" in product development crafted each of these publications, they gained valuable experience working in the new format. Everything learned from the comments and experiences just mentioned has been incorporated into the presentation of the TNIV now being published as *The Books of the Bible*. Our hope and prayer is that this edition will provide both new and returning readers of the Bible with a fresh, life-transforming encounter with the word of God.

HOW TO USE THIS EDITION

The Books of The Bible is designed, first and foremost, to be read, with both pleasure and understanding. This does not mean, however, that it should be left on the table by the easy chair for use in personal devotions while traditional chapter-and-verse versions are taken to church and Bible studies, and used for sermon and lesson preparation by preachers and teachers. Reading must be the ground discipline for any appropriation we wish to make of God's word. *The Books of The Bible*, therefore, as an edition formatted to be read, will be of value for the whole range of public and private uses we make of the Scriptures.

We may, however, need to readjust our ideas of what it means to "read" the Bible before we welcome the idea that this is what must undergird our every engagement with God's word. Our experience of Bible reading may have been conditioned by programs created to help us "get through" the Bible in a year—as if this were an onerous and burdensome task, best accomplished in short sessions over a long period of time. We may have followed a plan that assigned readings of a fixed length from both the Old Testament and the New Testament each day. Such plans have admittedly helped many people read the whole Bible who otherwise would not have. But not only do their assigned daily portions, like traditional chapters, often fail to correspond with natural literary divisions, they also require readers to jump back and forth between different books, at the expense of continuity and context.

For example, in one plan I saw recently, participants were assigned on their first day in the book of Deuteronomy to read as far as the point in the historical prologue where the Israelites defeat King Sihon. Leaving the conquest of the Transjordan to be completed the next day, readers were to finish their assignment by turning to the account of the Triumphal Entry in the gospel of Mark. The following day, they were to complete Deuteronomy's historical prologue and read the introduction to its covenant stipulations—but none of the stipulations themselves. Those, too, had to await another day while participants discovered, back in the gospel of Mark, what happened to the fig tree they heard Jesus curse the day before. In such a program it is difficult to avoid approaching the Scriptures as a series of brief, discrete devotional passages whose meaning consists in the coincidence of some striking phrase with whatever is on the reader's mind at the time.

The simple fact is that the reading the entire Bible does not represent a year's worth of hard slogging. If the average American simply gave up watching television and used that time to read the Scriptures instead, the whole Bible could be finished in just two weeks: Americans watch an average of 35 hours of television a week, and the Bible can be read in 70 hours. So the problem is not sheer volume of material. It is more likely the habits of reading that reliance on chapters and verses as guides to Scripture encourage. Those habits cause us to experience the biblical books as disintegrated, dry and confusing works. If we are not reading the Bible with pleasure and understanding, those 70 hours are going to be hard slogging whether we cover them in a year or in a fortnight.

How, then, should we read? The simplest way to put it is that we should *experience* the books of the Bible, just the way we would seek to experience any other literary, artistic or musical creation. Who would look at details from a painting without first standing back and gazing at the whole thing, engaging it with the aesthetic sensibilities, and not addressing it only with the analytical faculty? Would anyone really try to appreciate excerpts from a symphony without listening to it all the way through first, letting the voices of the different instruments swim through their heads and the composer's passion carry them away to heights and depths of sensibility? Earlier in this chapter the analogy of a DVD was offered to explain our group's decision to place all supporting materials outside the texts of the biblical books. DVDs can provide a further analogy here. They divide the films they present into "chapters" that can be accessed individually and which could conceivably be watched separately—even one a day. But it is hard to imagine anyone watching a film that way. Nor should anyone read a book of the Bible for the first time in fragments, even if the goal is eventually to study each of its parts in detail.

As Richard Moulton observed,

> The revelation which is the basis of our modern religion has been
> made in the form of literature. . . . And the best treatment for

this literature is to read it. For those who wish there exists a vast apparatus of all kinds of helps in Bible study. But let us not forget the subtle and besetting danger in all literary study—that the process of studying tends to eclipse the literature itself. Scholarship can do much for the Bible: but imagination and literary receptivity can do more.[12]

Or, as Sir Arthur Quiller-Couch put it succinctly in his celebrated lectures at Cambridge on *The Art of Reading*, "My first piece of advice 'on reading the Bible' is to do it."[13]

And once we have been able to experience a chosen book of the Bible as a whole work—letting it wash over us like a great literary wave—and the time comes to move beyond that foundational encounter to study and contemplation and analysis, we must recognize that we still cannot read smaller sections meaningfully without attaining an *intellectual* apprehension of the whole. In that endeavor we would do well to follow the advice given by Mortimer Adler and Charles van Doren in their classic volume *How to Read a Book*. They advise us to look for the answers to four key questions as we begin to study any new book:[14]

- What kind of book is this? Is it a novel, a textbook, a collection of poems, a biography? The kind or *literary genre* of book before us should determine our expectations in reading. For example, should it bother us

---

12. Richard Moulton, "Preface," *The Modern Reader's Bible* (New York: Macmillan, 1907), pp. vii, ix-x.

13. Arthur Quiller-Couch, "On Reading the Bible (I)," *The Art of Reading: Lectures Delivered in the University of Cambridge, 1916–1917* (Cambridge: University Press, 1920), http://www.bartleby.com/191/8.html.

14. Mortimer Adler and Charles van Doren, *How to Read a Book* (New York: MJF Books, 1972), pp. 59-95. In the authors' own words (p. 95):

"1. Classify the book according to kind and subject matter.

2. State what the whole book is about with the utmost brevity.

3. Enumerate its major parts in their order and relation, and outline these parts as you have outlined the whole.

4. Define the problem or problems the author is trying to solve." (I take these points up in a different order.)

if the author relates events that we doubt could really have happened? It shouldn't in a science fiction novel, but it should if we are reading the purportedly true account of an ascent of Mount Everest. (An excellent resource for recognizing and understanding the different genres represented in the pages of Scripture is *How to Read the Bible For All Its Worth* by Gordon Fee and Douglas Stuart.[15])

• Why was this book written? That is, what specific situation was the author speaking to? What problem or problems gave rise to the book in the first place? (This is the task of determining a book's *circumstances and occasion of composition.*)

• How is the book put together? What are the major parts, and into what smaller parts are these divided? When it comes to modern books, it is usually the case that the chapters and larger divisions correspond to the argument or story's essential parts, because these divisions are the work of the author. In the case of biblical books, however, we must always be mindful that the chapters and verses are not the work of the original authors, but were added centuries later. While they sometimes correspond to a biblical book's essential parts, they most often do not. So we must make it another piece of preliminary business to gain an understanding of a book's *literary structure.*

• Finally, we must ask what overall idea or purpose unites all of the parts and aspects of the book. This is the task of identifying and expressing its *thematic unity.*

It may be necessary to read all of the way through a book three or four times, looking for the answer to each of these questions in turn. With practice, it may become possible to answer all of the questions after a single reading. Even so, it remains true that we are not in a position to read smaller sections meaningfully until we have an appreciation of the whole. It was precisely this process, in fact, that we heard John Locke describe at the beginning of Chapter Three:

---

15.   Gordon D. Fee and Douglas Stuart, *How to Read the Bible For All Its Worth* (Grand Rapids: Zondervan, 1982).

I concluded it necessary, for the understanding of any one of St. Paul's epistles, to read it all through at one sitting; and to observe, as well as I could, the drift and design of his writing it. If the first reading gave me some light, the second gave me more; and so I persisted on, reading constantly the whole epistle over at once, till I came to have a good general view of the apostle's main purpose in writing the epistle, the chief branches of his discourse wherein he prosecuted it, the arguments he used, and the disposition of the whole. This, I confess, is not to be obtained by one or two hasty readings; it must be repeated again and again, with a close attention to the tenour of the discourse, and a perfect neglect of the divisions into chapters and verses.[16]

The introductions in *The Books of The Bible* are designed specifically to help readers answer the four preliminary questions we have just discussed. We have not used these introductions to draw contemporary applications of biblical teachings or to situate books within a larger systematic-theological framework. Our goal has been to help readers recognize what kind of book they are reading, how it is put together, why it was written and how it speaks to the situation that motivated it. We believe that, thus equipped, readers will understand the Scriptures better and enjoy them more. The Holy Spirit can then help them draw personal and contemporary applications from biblical books with which they are even more vitally engaged.

By now this may all sound very inviting, perhaps even exciting, but there may still be a concern: "What if I don't have time to read a whole book at once?" In response to this concern I would offer several observations.

First, when you sit down and actually *read* the Bible, you may surprise yourself. You may find what you are reading so interesting and engaging that you take the time to finish a book, and rearrange your schedule accordingly. As our format was being developed, I gave a sample that

---

16.   John Locke, "An Essay for the Understanding of St. Paul's Epistles, by Consulting St. Paul Himself," *The Works of John Locke*, 12th ed. (London: Rivington et al., 1824), 7: xiii. (Facsimile edition, http://oll.libertyfund.org/Home3/Book.php?recordID=0128.07.) This "perfect neglect," of course, will be much easier to cultivate in an edition in which chapter and verse numbers are removed from the text and margins.

included several biblical books to some of the college students who attend my church. Later in the week I heard one of them report to another, "I read right through the whole book of Galatians, because nothing told me to stop." She was referring to the absence of the large, bold chapter numbers that we typically (but often unadvisedly) take to signify, "You've just reached a meaningful pause in the book; stop and think about what you've read." That was one important factor. However, I think she also read through the whole book because something told her to keep going: the unfolding argument of the epistle. We make time for activities that we enjoy and consider meaningful, and a fresh experience of the Scriptures may lead us to make time for them that we might otherwise consider unavailable.

But suppose you really do not have time in your daily schedule to read whole books of the Bible at a sitting. Then read them when you do have the time. On a weekend, set aside an uninterrupted hour or two (it takes no longer than this to finish most biblical books) and go through the book that you wish to engage next, simply following the flow of its unfolding argument or narrative, or experiencing each of the songs or oracles in its collection in succession. Then, during the shorter periods you can set aside daily, begin formulating your answers to the questions of genre, structure, circumstances of composition and thematic unity. Refer back to the book to identify statements that confirm your developing understanding. You may want to record these in a topically arranged notebook. Or, you may mark and annotate them right in your Bible, perhaps using different colors for statements that relate to different questions. Once you have gotten a good feel for the book as a whole, perhaps reading it all the way through once or twice more, you can then engage its smaller sections meaningfully in the shorter sessions you will continue to have on most days.

For example, suppose you decide that you want to engage the book of Judges next. In the TNIV it contains around 16,600 words. The average adult reading speed has been estimated at between 200 and 300 words per minute. Thus it should take most readers between an hour and an hour a half to finish all of Judges. That would be a very engaging way to spend part of a rainy Saturday morning (although the task could also be accomplished on a weekday evening simply by foregoing two or three sitcoms). Now the book has been loaded into your mind and you can meditate on it "when you sit at home and when you travel along the road, when you lie down and when you get up" (as Moses said in Deuteronomy). By Monday morning, when you are heading off to work, or on Monday night, when you're winding down from a long day, you may find that you don't have another 60-90 minutes to spend in devotions. But you probably will have time and energy to begin recording your observations, checking back with the text to confirm your recollections.

For example, having realized that Judges is structurally a series of biographies, you may list all the judges in a notebook, or else circle the first occurrences of their names right in the text—let's say in blue. You may also have noticed that the phrase "again the Israelites did evil in the eyes of the LORD" introduces the stories of each of the six judges whose careers are described in some detail. You will choose underline this phrase in blue, too, since it also seems to relate to literary structure. But you might use black to underline the occurrences of the phrase "in those days Israel had no king" (or put a star next to them in the margin, or cite them in a separate section of your notebook), because they relate instead to the book's circumstances of composition: Judges was likely written to argue that Israel should have a king. And you might mark in red each of the features of the judges that makes them seem unlikely figures for God to work through in bringing deliverance. Gideon, for example, says he is the least in his family, and that his clan is the weakest in its tribe; Jephthah is an outcast because of his illegitimate birth; etc. These features point to one of the central themes of the book, that God brings deliverance by His own power, not necessarily through those in positions of earthly advantage.

Whatever method you use to record your observations, after some days you will have made most of your notes about the book as a whole. (These can always be supplemented later by further insights.) You can then use your shorter daily sessions to consider each of the parts of the book individually, studying, for example, the career of one judge, or a significant episode within a longer career. You will be able to reflect on this passage in detail with an appreciation for how it fits into the book as a whole and advances its overall designs. (The line spacing in *The Books of The Bible* is intended to help readers identify such smaller meaningful units within books. At the same time, however, it is meant to be unobtrusive so that it does not discourage or prevent readers from considering any units they choose.)

An appropriate exception to the general method of first understanding a book as a whole, and then understanding each of its parts in light of that whole, may be made in the case of biblical books that are not single literary compositions, but rather collections of compositions. While it is certainly neither the chapter nor the verse that is the significant unit for reading in the Bible, in some cases it may not be a book, either, but rather the individual compositions within it. The Bible contains some books that are largely collections: of lyric poems, for example, or of prophetic oracles and vision reports. Trying to read all the way through them at a single sitting may require plunging repeatedly into new compositions without letting the experience of previous ones settle in. And this could be psychologically and aesthetically wearying. So in the case of these books, it may be more satisfying to read their constituent compositions separately first, as many as you choose to engage at a sitting, and then, once you have read them all, to reflect on how the book as a whole has been assembled. You will answer the four investigative questions about the book by drawing on information acquired during your reading of its individual compositions. You will then be in a position to consider how its parts have taken on a broader meaning as members of a larger collection. In other words, if you read a collection composition by composition, the movement will be first from the parts to the whole, and then, as in the case of books that represent single compositions, from the whole back to the parts.

Using *The Books of The Bible* for personal devotions following this approach should make your times of Scripture reading and meditation more enjoyable and meaningful. They will keep you coming back for more, and as you do, you will be storing up the word of God in your mind and heart, where the Holy Spirit can use it to speak to you right away, or in a month, or in a year. The goal is not to find a "thought for the day" in some phrase that strikes you within each day's passage (although you may find God speaking to you that way on occasion). The goal is to come to know the Scriptures better and better, so that as you pursue Christian maturity, you will make decisions and respond to challenges and questions with biblical wisdom, within the framework of a biblical world view. And even beyond this, you will come to recognize the scope and grandeur of the story that the Bible tells, and see where you can take your place in that story as it continues down to our day and beyond.

The principles just illustrated with approaches to devotional reading will also allow *The Books of The Bible* to be used in preparation for preaching and teaching. This edition, in fact, should prove a valuable primary resource for those activities, even though Bibles with chapters and verses will likely continue to have a secondary role in some specialized applications related to them. Chapters and verses, it will be recalled, were originally introduced so that scholarly resources such as commentaries and concordances could be created, and they will remain useful as the system to which such resources have been keyed. (One system or another had to be developed for them to have been created at all.)

For example, in my own sermon preparation each week, I begin by considering a passage in the original language and by "establishing the text" using a critical edition of the Old or New Testament that allows me to compare readings from various manuscripts. Chapters and verses are not strictly necessary for translation, but if I want to get a feel for a given term by exploring how it is used in other contexts, I will turn to a Greek or Hebrew lexicon or concordance, and it will send me to those other contexts via the traditional numbering system. Chapters and verses are not really needed for textual criticism, either. All of the leading critical texts[17] use footnotes to indicate where textual variations

---

17. E.g. The United Bible Societies, *The Greek New Testament*, 4th rev. ed. (Stuttgart: Deutsche Bibelgesellschaft, 1994); *Novum Testamentum Graece*, 27th ed.

occur, signalling them with numbers, letters or symbols. Nevertheless, if I am considering various textual-critical choices and want to read an assessment of their respective merits, I will open a textual commentary that is organized by book, chapter and verse. So Bibles with these traditional divisions marked within the text will remain useful for some specialized purposes.

Even so, chapters and verses are beginning to get some stiff competition from electronic alternatives, which are rapidly reducing the number of tasks that actually require recourse to them. When I am looking for the exact wording of a statement in the Bible, I rarely reach over to my bookshelf to pull out a concordance and flip through its pages to find a key word listing that will give me a chapter and verse reference I must then look up. I am much more likely to do a string search on an Internet site such as BibleGateway (which is literally at my fingertips, through my computer keyboard, and already bookmarked on my browser). By this means the statement is displayed for me in a single step—and I have not had to rely on the medieval numbering system at all. Similarly, all the major Bible reference works are now widely available in CD-ROM format, in which electronic string searches can be performed.

But whether we use such electronic resources, or continue to rely on the many helpful reference works that have been created over the years geared to the chapter and verse system, we must always remember that chapters and verses were not intended as guides to reading. However we might use them in specialized tasks, they should no longer dictate our reading habits. And an alert, inquisitive reading such as we have already encouraged for private devotions must be the ground discipline for using a biblical book as the basis for a sermon series, Bible study or adult class. (It is irresponsible to teach or preach from a *book* you have not *read!*) The four preliminary questions discussed above should be answered in the teacher or preacher's mind from an engaged reading of

---

(Stuttgart: Deutsche Bibelgesellschaft, 1993); *Biblical Hebraica Stuttgartensia*, 4th ed. (Stuttgart: Deutsche Bibelgesellschaft, 1990).

the whole text before individual passages are considered. In fact, a sermon, study or lecture on each question would provide an excellent introduction to the presentations that would follow on the individual passages within the book. And all participants should be encouraged to read the entire book themselves, as part of their preparation for the study or series.

One summer, for example, I led a Bible study on Colossians for about twenty college students. A few days before our first session, I e-mailed each of them the entire text of the book (with chapter and verse numbers removed) and asked them to read through it looking for the answers to the following questions, all relating to circumstances of composition:

• Who wrote this letter? Where was the author when he wrote? (How much of the letter did its author actually set down on paper?)

• To whom was this letter written? What can we tell about the addressees? (e.g. Were they Jews or Gentiles? etc.)

• Had the author and the addressees ever met? If so, where and when and how did they meet? If not, who or what established a connection between them? Who delivered the letter?

• Why did the author write to the addressees? Can you pick out one phrase from the letter that epitomizes the purpose for which it was written? What else can you find in the text that sheds light on the circumstances and occasion of its writing?

When the students gathered for our first meeting, they had found clear answers to all of these questions and could support them by reference to the text. We devoted a second session to discussing the literary structure of Colossians, appreciating how this reflected the conventions of the epistolary genre. Afterwards I sent them all a new copy of the letter in which the sections they had identified and described were marked. Only then did we take up these sections one at a time, each week deepening our understanding of the epistle's underlying themes. I have always felt that the keen interest the students showed right through the summer reflected their appreciation for an approach that was much more meaningful than a "chapter by chapter" study would likely have been. (I must also admit, however, that the desserts my wife made for the group as it gathered in our home each week also had to have been a strong draw; her chocolate raspberry trifle was particularly well received.) *The Books of The Bible* has been designed specifically to encourage such respectful and engaging approaches to the study and teaching of the Scriptures.

However, readers of the Bible in its traditional format will need to adopt some new habits in order to benefit fully from such an edition, particularly as they bring it into contexts where approaches geared to what I have called our "habit of not reading" are still being followed. One question we have been asked from the start of our project is, "How will I find my place?" Many readers of the Bible count on being able to find statements readily within the Scriptures when they are cited by speakers, teachers or authors by book, chapter and verse. With the elimination of numbering from the text and a change in book order, will locating citations now become so cumbersome and time-consuming that the effort will simply be abandoned, and will God's word be read even less than before?

I don't think so. With just a little experience, statements can be found just as quickly when the Scriptures are presented in a format such as *The Books of The Bible* as they can be in the traditional format. There are only two short steps to follow.

The first is to find the book. I must note, from my eighteen years in the pastorate, that it is a rare person in most churches today who knows the traditional sequence of the books of the Bible by memory. (In one of my parishes a twelve year old girl learned the customary order as a school assignment. She recited it aloud in our worship sharing time and then challenged anyone else in the church to match the feat. Everyone else present declined, and all eyes turned to me, with congregational respect for my teaching authority apparently hanging in the balance. I am grateful to report that I was able to run through the list myself, and that I served many more years in that pulpit.)

I most often see people locating individual books within the Bible by opening to what they think is the general vicinity of the book they're looking for and rapidly flipping the pages until its title appears at the top of one of them. Otherwise, they will turn to the table of contents. (Most published Bibles today include a table of contents with the books in alphabetical order, a tacit acknowledgment that many readers are not likely to find a book by its place in the traditional sequence.) There should be absolutely no difference between looking up a book on the contents page of *The Books of The Bible* and looking it up on the contents page of any other edition. On the other hand, once the logic of the new book order has been internalized, books will be found by turning to them more directly, by reference to their placement ("oh yes, Paul wrote to the Thessalonians early in his ministry"). By this means books will be located just as quickly, and much more meaningfully, than they would be found through rote memorization of the traditional sequence.

The only other step in finding a statement identified by book, chapter and verse is to locate the statement itself within the book. In our edition, its chapter and verse reference will fall within one of the ranges provided at the bottom of each page. The reader can then scan the appropriate page to find the words being quoted by a speaker or writer. I have some friends who have been using their copy of the Preview Edition for what they call a "take to church Bible" ever since they received it. They report that they are able to find the weekly Scripture lesson just as quickly as those sitting around them—on many occasions, even faster. (In fact, in the churches I have served that had pew Bibles, it was expected that the Scripture lesson would be listed in the bulletin by page number as well as by book, chapter and verse. Many of my parishioners told me that they would not be able to find it otherwise.)

This two-step approach admittedly does not work when only a reference is provided and the statement is not then read aloud. However, this is a practice that should simply not be accepted in public teaching. I hope that none of my parishioners would ever sit still for my saying something like, "And so we should read the Bible every day, as Acts 17:11 tells us to." This leaves the listener with the unfortunate choice of scrambling to verify the statement and missing much of what is said in the meantime, or else just trusting that what the speaker has said expresses a genuine biblical teaching—which Acts 17:11 tells us not to do! ("They . . . examined the Scriptures every day to see if what Paul said was true.")

Biblical statements that are cited in printed works by reference only are a different matter. The writer may be constrained by a word count or page limit that prevents frequent verbatim quotations, and the reader presumably has the leisure to look up the statement without missing what is said next. But in either speaking or writing, if time or space allow, why not quote the words? For that matter, why put people in the uncomfortable position of having to look up a reference hurriedly at all? Today's technologies make this unnecessary.

In the churches I have attended recently that have had central viewing screens in their sanctuaries, the Scripture lesson has always been displayed on the screen while being read aloud. (This has typically been without inserted verse numbers, I have been interested to note.) In my own churches (which, I will admit, have been a little behind the curve in terms of widescreen technological innovation), I have sometimes had the Scripture lesson printed in its entirety in the bulletin. Or I have sent it out in advance in my weekly e-mail newsletter. But if a church adopted *The Books of The Bible* as its sanctuary Bible, making it available to all attendees in the seats or pews, the lesson could simply be listed by page number, where it would be found quickly as soon as it began to be read aloud.

In a group study using *The Books of The Bible*, a leader or participant could easily bring particular statements within a passage to everyone's attention by quoting their opening words, or by describing their place in the passage. (Statements should not be identified by their position on the page, however: "It's in the paragraph about a third of the way down, no, not that one, the one after it . . .") I recently took part in a study of the book of Amos using a text without chapters and verses. The members quickly caught on to how they could say things like, "That same idea is expressed in the oracle against Gaza at the start of the book" rather than, much less meaningfully, "Chapter one, verse six says the same thing." Indeed, while chapters and verses do provide quick access to statements within Scripture, in many cases they provide too quick access, as statements may be found without regard to their context and thus considered independently of the meaning they have in that context.

In short, "How will I find my place?" is really an artificial problem. Even users of traditional Bibles should not wait until the last minute to look up the morning's Scripture lesson in worship, when a glance at the bulletin upon entering the sanctuary would enable them to mark the passage at their leisure and turn to it without scrambling when it was announced. Anyone who had brought *The Books of The Bible* to church could find the appropriate page upon entering as well. With a little fore-thought by both students and teachers, speakers and hearers, a text under consideration can be made available to everyone without occasioning a sword-drill style dash through the pages of the Bible.

"How will I find my place without chapters and verses?" A final question to ask in response is, "How will you find your place *with* them?" As noted earlier, the Bible relates the ongoing story of how God has been working in the world to restore harmony within humanity and the creation by reconciling them to Himself. It invites us to find our own place in this story and join in this work of God. But how will we ever do that if the only version of the story we have ever encountered is frag-mented and disjointed, presented as a chapter here and a verse there? We need to experience the full sweep of the story of God's work, to feel ourselves being drawn to take our own part in it, and to accept that invitation through faith and obedience. The greatest danger of wanting quick access to discrete statements in the Bible is that this may be all we ever hear in its pages: discrete statements, not a story that has a role in it for us, just waiting to be accepted.

It is therefore my personal hope that *The Books of The Bible* will not only be well received as an individual edition, but that it will help reshape our understanding of how the Scriptures may most effectively be presented. I hope that, as new formats come to be more widely employed, multitudes of readers will have the opportunity to engage God's word with greater understanding and enjoyment, and thus find their places in His ongoing work in our world.

APPENDIX

HOW LITERARY STRUCTURES WERE IDENTIFIED

In Chapter Three the distinction was drawn between how the larger literary structures of each of the biblical books could be *indicated*, and how they were to be *identified* in the first place. Having discussed the first question in that chapter, it is time to address the second one here.

Within the Bible Design Group, I was given the assignment of identifying the literary structures that would be represented in *The Books of The Bible*. I was given this task because over the years I had already investigated the structures of many individual books and in the process had developed and refined an approach that I felt could be taken to the books of the Bible in general. We felt that the consistent use of a single method would provide a more harmonious presentation for readers than the use of different means to determine the literary structure of different books.

In my own personal research and in my work for the Bible Design Group, I began with an authority commitment: the belief that the Bible is the inspired word of God, and more specifically that its inspiration resides on the level of authorial intent, not on the level of plain words that might be taken to mean a number of things.[1] I therefore proceeded in the belief that just as we seek to discover authors' intentions in order to understand the meaning of individual biblical passages, so our understanding of any biblical book's structure must also be informed by a search for the author's expressed literary-structural intentions. Indeed, since we should be guided in our understanding of the meaning of a given passage by an appreciation for the structure that provides its literary context, we must look to authors for direction on the matter of overarching structure as an essential part of our efforts to interpret individual passages.

The search for indications that the biblical authors may have given us of their literary-structural intentions has good prospects of success. Ancient writers did not have the freedom to add spacing and headings that abundant, affordable publishing materials now permit modern authors to use to indicate their outlines. Moreover, in many cases ancient works were intended to be delivered orally, and were written down only for transmission to their recipients. (Note, for example, Paul's admonition to the Colossians: "After this letter has been read to you, see that it is also read in the church of the Laodiceans.") For both of these reasons, it has long seemed reasonable to me that ancient authors would have embedded recognizable literary-structural signals directly within their works.

I became convinced, after many years of research and reflection, that within the pages of the Bible these signals characteristically take the form of recurring phrases and references that have been placed intentionally at the seams of literary structures. One way of confirming that they are likely being employed to signal structural transitions (and are

---

1.   There are other levels on which the Bible's inspiration is held to reside besides these two. An excellent discussion is found in Gabriel Fackre, *The Christian Story: A Pastoral Systematics, Volume 2, Authority: Scripture in the Church for the World* (Grand Rapids: Eerdmans, 1987), pp. 60-91. Fackre documents further views such as, for example, those that the Bible is authoritative in that it is a witness to the "acts of God" in salvation history, or because it is a means through which one may encounter Christ.

not just favorite expressions that authors like to use) is to recognize how their appearances coincide with structural seams that may be identified more implicitly from other characteristics of a work such as shifts in genre, changes in topic or progression of plot.

In the preceding pages we have already encountered several examples of how book structure is likely indicated by such recurring phrases. In Chapter One, for instance, it was noted that many of the groups of laws in Leviticus conclude with a standard summary formula, "These are the regulations" (*zo'th torath* or *zo'th hattorah l-*). The use of this formula makes explicit a structure that may already be recognized implicitly from the book's topical ordering principle. We noted similarly in Chapter Three that Paul introduces many of his topical discussions in 1 Corinthians with summary statements that begin "now about" (*peri de*), and that in Genesis a new phase of the narrative relating to the progeny of the next significant figure is consistently introduced by the phrase "this is the account of" (*'elleh toledoth*). And we saw in Chapter Two that the successive reigns described in Samuel-Kings are introduced or concluded by a standard formula that gives a king's name and lineage and enumerates his years on the throne.

But the phrases by which biblical authors point to structural transitions may be integrated more directly into their works than this. In Chapter One, for example, we also saw how variations on the phrase "when Jesus had finished saying these things" come right after each of five long discourses in Matthew. (After the last one the wording is, appropriately, "when Jesus had finished saying *all* these things."[2]) The structural significance of these phrases is suggested by the way they all occur at transitions between discourse and narrative. But unlike the more obvious summary statements in Leviticus, 1 Corinthians,

---

2. Similarly, at the end of each of the sections of the so-called "Book of Signs" in the first half of John, there is a reference to belief or unbelief in Jesus; at the end of the last section, John writes, "Even after Jesus had performed *so many signs* in their presence, they still would not believe in him." See John 2:11, 4:53, 5:47, 6:69, 10:19-21, 10:42 and 12:37.

Genesis and Samuel-Kings, these are built right into the resuming narrative of the gospel itself.

The case is the same with the formula from the book of Judges that we noted in Chapter Three and Chapter Four, "Again the Israelites did evil in the eyes of the LORD." While this statement, too, is made within the narrative, it always comes as a new judge is about to be introduced. It thus marks a literary-structural seam in a book that is essentially organized biographically, and it does so without the narrator having to step outside the story.

Examples of other similarly embedded structural indicators may readily be provided from other books of the Bible.[3] A variation of the benediction "Praise be to the LORD, the God of Israel, from everlasting to everlasting, Amen and Amen" occurs between each of the five sections into which Psalms has been divided. These benedictions have come to be treated as the endings of the last psalms in each section; they have even been numbered as the last verse of these psalms, even though in some cases they are quite incongruous. Psalm 89, for example, is a lament that would end quite surprisingly with a burst of praise if the benediction were its real conclusion. But this traditional assimilation of the benedictions into the preceding psalms simply indicates how successfully these

---

3.   It will be noted that in the following examples from Psalms and the prophetic collections, the literary-structural signals were likely provided by editors or compilers, not by the authors whose songs, oracles, etc. have been gathered together. If inspiration indeed resides on the level of authorial intent, should structures created and indicated by editors be considered as authoritative as those of authors? Put another way, could the contents of the biblical collections be rearranged with no loss to divinely inspired literary-structural intent? This is an interesting and complicated question that I do not have the space to discuss in detail here. It does seem to me that those books whose literary-structural signals are the work of their authors at least provide a model for understanding how editors, too, have indicated the structures they have created, and that this can help us interpret the biblical collections in the form in which we have received them. Whether interpreters would recommend any internal rearrangements based on authorial considerations would depend on the degree of authority they assigned to the tradition that has brought these books to us in their present shape.

structural dividers have been integrated into the liturgical material of the book.

Phrases that signal literary structure have also apparently been worked into the biblical collections of prophetic oracles. The book of Zephaniah has three main parts, which are distinguished topically: prophecies about the world-wide "day of the LORD"; oracles against individual nations; and promises of restoration to Israel. The first part ends, "In the fire of his jealousy the whole earth will be consumed [*be'esh qine'atho te'akel kol-ha'erets*], for he will make a sudden end of all who live on the earth." Even though the second part of the book concerns individual nations, it returns to a worldwide perspective at its very end and it concludes with a phrase that is repeated almost verbatim from the first part of the book: "The whole world will be consumed by the fire of my jealous anger [*be'esh qine'athi te'akel kol-ha'erets*]."

The book of Jeremiah, to cite another example, contains four large collections of materials. The first and the last contain mostly poetic oracles; they come from various times throughout the prophet's career. The middle two collections consist largely of biographical narratives from the later part of Jeremiah's life. In other words, these collections are distinct both in genre and in historical provenance. This distinction within the book, which can already be recognized implicitly by these considerations, seems to be signaled explicitly and intentionally (indeed, self-consciously) by the way each section ends with a reference to Jeremiah's words being written down in a book or on a scroll.[4]

Many more examples could be given. But this is not the place to offer an extensive account of the literary-structural signals I believe the biblical authors have sent us in the pages of their works. (The introductions in *The Books of The Bible* describe recurring phrases and references that occur at the seams of other books besides those already noted.) My present purpose is simply to explain that a consistent

---

4.   See Jeremiah 25:13, 36:32, 45:1 and 51:60. The one other such reference in the book (30:1-2) comes at the start of the oracle about the new covenant, which has been given a central place in the collection.

method was followed in identifying the literary structures that would be indicated in our edition: preference was given to interpretations in which phrases that were understood to reflect authorial intent to signal literary structure appeared at the boundaries between macrostructural units in outlines that were already discernible implicitly from a book's other characteristics.

Looking to such signals as guides to literary structure is admittedly not the only possible approach. Indeed, there is an active debate among scholars using a variety of methods as to the macrostructures of many biblical books. We in the Bible Design Group recognize that this scholarly conversation is in progress; through the publication of *The Books of The Bible*, we wish to join it. We feel that the method we have used to identify literary structures has already proven valuable for our purposes. In many cases it has largely confirmed analyses offered by others, and in some instances it has pointed the way to what we feel are fruitful avenues for future investigation.

Nevertheless, all of the interpretations we are suggesting are offered to readers and students of the Scriptures in a spirit of exploration. We acknowledge that reading itself is a creative act. Through the publication of this edition, we wish to share the beauty that we have come to see in the literary forms of the biblical books, and thereby to encourage Scripture reading with more enjoyment and understanding. We hope that our observations will be tested critically by scholars and other devoted readers of the Bible. If, in certain cases, some other analysis suggests a more reasonable account of the authors' intentions, we will gratefully draw on this demonstration to improve our own understanding of the Scriptures. But we do believe, nevertheless, that the method we have been pursuing does offer considerable promise in identifying the biblical authors' literary-structural designs, and so we are eager to share the results of our explorations to date.

It is valuable to recognize that while scholarly accounts of the macrostructures of individual biblical books do vary, the actual structures identified by individual interpreters are not necessarily as divergent as might first appear. Even when scholars use different methods and suggest contrasting thematic outlines, in the end they may divide a book into almost the same sections as others do. And because *The Books of The Bible* contains no section headings, its indications of macrostructure can thus be accommodated within a broad range of interpretations that are still in conversation with one another. In other words, it is not actually necessary to accept that authors' literary-structural intentions have been reliably identified through recurring phrases, or even to believe that authors have sent any intentional signals within their works at all, in order to be comfortable with the basic outlines of the literary structures we are indicating.

For example, in *How to Read the Bible Book By Book* (a volume that was, as I have noted, a valuable and influential resource for our project), Gordon Fee and Douglas Stuart write that 2 Corinthians is "probably two letters . . . combined into one," that is, a conflation of two letters that Paul wrote on separate occasions. They provide the following outline of its contents:

Salutation and Praise to God (1:1-11)

Explanation of Paul's Change of Plans (1:12-2:13)

Paul, Minister of the New Covenant (2:14-7:4)

The Explanation Renewed (7:5-16)

Have the Collection Ready When I Come (8:1-9:15)

Defense of Paul's Ministry against False Apostles (10:1-13:14)

They identify the last section specifically as likely derived from a different letter from the rest of the book as we now know it.[5]

The introduction in *The Books of The Bible*, by contrast, asserts the literary integrity of 2 Corinthians as an epistle composed entirely on a single occasion. In terms of structure, following an interpretation that Aída Besançon Spencer and William David Spencer offer in their commentary on the book, Paul is understood to address the Corinthians from a series of perspectives that correspond to geographic locations:

---

5.   Gordon Fee and Douglas Stuart, *How to Read the Bible Book by Book* (Grand Rapids: Zondervan, 2002), pp. 333-339.

Paul narrates this letter not along topics or themes. Rather, he uses a chronological schema and inserts along the way theological truths that these different events teach. In 1:3-11, Paul speaks of the troubles in Asia and what they taught about comfort and suffering. In 1:15-17 he speaks of his plans to go to Macedonia, and the importance of trust and love. In 2:12-13 he moves to Troas, a seaport town in Asia across from Macedonia, and discusses the truths he learned there. In 7:5-7 he has now crossed the Aegean Sea into Macedonia and found Titus. In 8:17 Paul begins to envision future travel south into the province of Achaia. In 10:2 he envisions his entrance into Corinth itself. Second Corinthians might thus be understood as a motion picture or a talk, illustrated by a map of the Mediterranean countries, which is periodically halted to explain what was happening in the participants' minds at each place.[6]

In keeping with this interpretation, the structural transitions in the epistle are considered in *The Books of The Bible* to be signaled by certain of these place references. The following outline is thus marked (using line spacing only; headings are provided here just for descriptive purposes):

Epistolary Opening and Thanksgiving (1:1-7)

Paul in Asia: If I make you sad, who can make me happy? (1:8-2:11)

Paul in Troas: Treasure in earthen vessels (2:12-7:4)

Paul in Macedonia: Working together again (7:5-9:15)

Paul in Corinth: Are they servants of Christ? I am more. (10:1-13:10)

Epistolary Closing (13:11-14)

This account of the book's structure would initially appear to differ significantly from the one offered by Fee and Stuart. This should not be surprising, since it reflects a contrasting interpretation of the book's circumstances of composition. However, upon closer inspection, the

---

6.   Aída Besançon Spencer and William David Spencer, *Bible Study Commentary: 2 Corinthians* (Grand Rapids: Lamplighter Books, 1989), pp. 54-55. The Spencers actually divide their own book into chapters according to a topical outline, however, illustrating that interpretations of literary structure can be in conversation with one another even within the same commentary.

differences prove to be quite minor, at least in terms of how the book is divided into sections.

Both outlines acknowledge that 2 Corinthians begins with some standard epistolary conventions; they diverge only in how they treat Paul's transition from these conventions into the epistle proper. *The Books of The Bible* considers the main body of the letter to begin when Paul starts addressing the Corinthians directly ("We do not want you to be uninformed"), while Fee and Stuart understand the conventional doxology to continue through Paul's references to prayer and thanksgiving. In both outlines the third section of the book is virtually the same; Fee and Stuart simply begin their section one Greek sentence later than we do. Their fourth and fifth sections, if taken together, coincide exactly with the fourth section in our edition. And the only other difference is that we have set off the brief epistolary closing elements as a distinct section, just as both outlines set off the opening ones. In other words, even when interpreted from varying perspectives, this epistle still "reads" very much the same way structurally.

The sections into which George Campbell divided Matthew in his 1778 translation of the gospels may provide the basis for another useful comparison. (As we saw in Chapter Three, Alexander Campbell used this translation in *The Sacred Writings,* incorporating its section headings into the text.) The translator divided this gospel into sixteen parts, based on major events in the narrative:[7]

I   The Nativity (1:1-2:23)

II   The Immersion (3:1-4:25)

III   The Sermon on the Mount (5:1-7:28)

IV   Several Miracles (8:1-9:34)

V   The Charge to the Apostles (9:35-11:1)

VI   The Character of the Times (11:2-12:50)

VII   Parables (13:1-53)

---

7.   See Alexander Campbell, *The Sacred Writings of the Apostles and Evangelists of Jesus Christ, Commonly Styled the New Testament* (1826; Nashville: Gospel Advocate Restoration Reprints, 2001), pp. 57-105.

VIII The People Twice Fed in the Desert (13:54-16:12)

IX   The Transfiguration (16:13-18:35)

X   The Rich Man's Application (19:1-20:16)

XI   The Entry Into Jerusalem (20:17-22:14)

XII   The Character of the Pharisees (22:15-23:39)

XIII The Prophecy on Mount Olivet (24:1-25:46)

XIV   The Last Supper (26:1-56)

XV   The Crucifixion (26:56-27:56)

XVI   The Resurrection (27:52-28:20)

Once again, this outline would appear at first to be very different from the one offered in *The Books of The Bible*. There, following the interpretation I summarized in Chapter One, Matthew is understood to have at its core (between the genealogy and the passion narrative) five "books," narrative-discourse pairs that each develop a shared theme relating to the kingdom of heaven.

But in this case as well, the two perspectives on literary structure are actually quite harmonious. Significantly, in Campbell's outline, each of the repetitions of the phrase "when Jesus had finished saying these things" comes either at the very end or the very beginning of a section. In other words, he, too, seems to have considered these phrases to be indicators of literary structure. When his sections are set alongside the units in the interpretation of Matthew's structure followed in our edition, the essential similarity of the two outlines becomes evident:

The Books of the Bible	Campbell's Translation
Genealogy + Foundations Narrative	I + II
Foundations Discourse	III
Mission Narrative	IV
Mission Discourse	V
Mystery Narrative	VI
Mystery Discourse	VII
Family Narrative + Family Discourse	VIII + IX
Destiny Narrative	X + XI + XII
Destiny Discourse	XIII
Passion Narrative	XIV + XV + XVI

George Campbell, we should note, included the transitional passage 9:35-38 with the charge to the disciples at the start of Section V; in a few other cases, he assigned transitional sentences to earlier or later sections than in our outline. But beyond these incidental differences, the sections compared here are exact matches. Given such examples, we hope it will be recognized that the structural outlines marked without headings in *The Books of The Bible* actually embrace a broad range of underlying interpretations within the scholarly conversation.[8]

It should be observed further that because *The Books of The Bible* is a presentation of Today's New International Version, the members of the Committee on Bible Translation had already determined how the *microstructures* of the biblical books would be represented. These translators divided the text into sentences and paragraphs, and we respected their work in every case. This had an indirect influence on the decisions we made regarding how to represent *macrostructure*, since no interpretations could be followed that would have required placing a break within a sentence or paragraph.

In fact, the work of the Committee reached into higher levels of literary structure in some places. The TNIV includes section headings that are intended as an aid to the reader, but which are not meant to be regarded as part of the biblical text. TNIV Bibles may be published without these headings, but if they are omitted, the translators have specified that at certain points spacing must be left where headings

---

8.   This is true on a higher level of literary organization as well. There has not been wide scholarly discussion of how the extended narrative in Genesis through Kings, if taken as a whole, should then be subdivided. But we may observe that if Moulton, who did pursue this question, had simply kept 1 Samuel together with the rest of Samuel-Kings (as I argued in Chapter Three he reasonably might have), this would have aligned his divisions quite neatly with the recombinations and groupings now being suggested in *The Books of The Bible*: Genesis; Exodus, Leviticus and Numbers; Deuteronomy; Joshua and Judges; Ruth; Samuel-Kings. In other words, there is really no great divergence between our understanding of appropriate biblical book boundaries within this extended narrative and that reflected in the work of a thoughtful interpreter one hundred years ago.

would otherwise appear. Many of these spaces preserve distinctions of genre: they set off legal, lyrical, genealogical or epistolary material that appears within a larger narrative. But in a few places they seem to express interpretations of macrostructure. Spaces are required before the occurrences of the phrase "this is the account of" in Genesis, for example. Once again, we respected these indications in every instance, so that the collective wisdom of the Committee exerted a further indirect influence on the representation of macrostructure in *The Books of The Bible*. (Nevertheless, it should be stated clearly that this presentation of the TNIV is not the work of the Committee on Bible Translation, but of the Bible Design Group, which is solely responsible for it.)

In the end, as great works of literature, many biblical books may be so complex and beautiful in form as to admit multiple perspectives on their literary structures. We therefore do not wish to assert that the interpretations embodied in *The Books of The Bible* are definitive. But we are convinced that this edition does offer a reasonable account of literary structure for each of the biblical books. Interpreters will no doubt continue to disagree on structural details, both small and large. But there should be general agreement that encountering the Bible in a clean, plain text, with reasonable structural outlines subtly suggested, will in any event be more profitable to readers than continuing to use chapters and verses as guides to the Scriptures.

Because we wished to honor the ongoing scholarly conversation about the literary structure of many biblical books, we recognized that in the preparation of our edition we needed to proceed humbly, with an openness to all of the insights that could be obtained from the broader scholarly community. We resolved to be receptive to the comments and even criticisms our edition might attract, and to keep it "evergreen," always open for future revision. But at the same time, we felt an urgency about our task that made us willing to commit to the interpretations we are presenting now. As we state in the Preface to *The Books of The Bible:*

> Just as the work of Bible translation is never finished, the work of
> formatting the Bible on the principles described here will never be

completed. Advances in the literary interpretation of the biblical books will undoubtedly enable the work we have begun here to be extended and improved in the years ahead. Yet the need to help readers overcome the many obstacles inherent in the Bible's current format is urgent, so we humbly offer the results of our work to those seeking an improved visual presentation of its sacred books.[9]

---

9.   The Bible Design Group, "Preface," *The Books of The Bible: A Presentation of Today's New International Version* (Colorado Springs: International Bible Society, 2007), p. vi.

Acknowledgments

I am grateful to acknowledge the generous and indispensable assistance of many friends in the creation of this book. Members of the Williams Christian Fellowship, the First Baptist Church of Williamstown and the University Baptist Church of East Lansing welcomed sermons, Bible studies and adult classes that did not seek to access the Bible through the traditional chapter and verse system. They thus provided a living laboratory in which I could develop the approach to Scripture described in this book. The Regent College Summer School invited me to teach a course in 1999 on "The Bible Without Chapters and Verses" and so gave me the opportunity to consolidate my research and reflections. The students in that course helped me refine my thinking through their questions, comments and papers. I appreciate the opportunity I was offered to give a public lecture at the Summer School. The positive response of the many who attended demonstrated the interest, even enthusiasm, that accompanies the realization of how much beauty lies in God's word, behind the mask of traditional elements. Many from the Summer School encouraged me to turn my lectures into a book. I appreciate this encouragement, which led to my writing an early version, entitled *The Bible Without Chapters and Verses: Exploring Scripture's Inherent Designs,* and posting it on the Internet. I am grateful to Jim and Judy Oraker for calling this book to Glenn Paauw's attention, and to Glenn for inviting me to become part of the Bible Design Group. During our four years of working together, all the members of that group—Glenn Paauw, Gene Rubingh, John Kohlenberger, John Dunham, Paul Berry, Micah Weiringa, Lisa Anderson and Jim Rottenborn—shared ideas and observations with me and asked insightful and fruitful questions. Members of the Committee on Bible Translation and leaders of the Bible divisions at Zondervan offered both cautionary and encouraging advice to our group, and this advice has helped shape my presentation here. Rob Clements of Clements Publishing in Toronto worked very patiently and helpfully with a book project that was on again, off again for some time until finally moving forward. Micah Weiringa read through much of the draft of this book with great care and attention to detail, addressing issues as small as an italicized footnote number and as large as the themes of the work as a whole. Glenn Paauw also read much of the draft and offered valuable suggestions. Simon Ahn proofread the typeset book quickly and accurately. Many friends undergirded us in prayer and helped see the manuscript through to completion. Words cannot express my gratitude to my beloved wife and lifelong ministry partner Priscilla, who has always been my greatest supporter. I particularly appreciate the understanding she showed of the demands that the writing of this book placed on my time and attention. And supremely I give thanks to God, who has "blessed us in the heavenly realms with every spiritual blessing in Christ." One of the greatest of the blessings we have received in this life is surely the gift of His word. May we appreciate its truth and beauty more each day. As George Herbert wrote, "Thy word is all, if we could spell."

Printed in the United States
84936LV00003B/280-321/A